Move On

Study Guide

Move On

When Mercy Meets Your Mess

Vicki Courtney

W PUBLISHING GROUP

AN IMPRINT OF THOMAS NELSON

Published in Nashville, Tennessee, by W Publishing, an imprint of Thomas Nelson.

Published in association with the literary agency of D.C. Jacobson & Associates LLC, an Author Management Company. www.dcjacobson.com

Thomas Nelson titles may be purchased in bulk for educational, business, fund-raising, or sales promotional use. For information, please e-mail SpecialMarkets@ThomasNelson.com.

ISBN 978-0-849-96006-2

First Printing June 2014 / Printed in the United States of America

Contents

How to Use This Guide

Group Size

The *Move On: When Mercy Meets Your Mess* video-based curriculum is designed to be experienced in a group setting such as a Bible study, Sunday school class, or any small group gathering. After viewing the video together, members will participate in a group discussion. Ideally, this group should be no larger than fifteen people. If the total number of participants in your group is much larger, consider breaking into two or more groups.

Materials Needed

Each participant should have her own study guide, which includes video teaching questions, small group discussion questions, and daily personal studies to deepen learning between sessions.

Facilitation

Each group should appoint a facilitator who is responsible for starting the video and for keeping track of time during discussions and activities. Facilitators may also read questions aloud and monitor discussions, prompting participants to respond and ensuring that everyone has the opportunity to participate.

Between-Sessions Personal Study

You can maximize the impact of the curriculum with additional study between the group sessions. Carving out about two hours total for personal study between meeting times will enable you to complete the between-session studies by the end of the six sessions. For each session, you may wish to complete the personal study all in one sitting or to spread it out over a few days (for example, working on it for a half-hour a day on four different days that week). If you are unable to finish (or even start!) your between-sessions study, still attend the group study video session! We are all busy and life happens. You are still wanted and welcome at class, even if you don't have your "homework" done.

A Note from Vicki

Dear friend,

I thought about adding a warning label on this study guide that states it is not for the "faint at heart." I realize that's not a very good sales pitch to get women to do this study, but it's true. Regardless of the circumstances, moving on can be a difficult task. We are a stubborn people, and many of us have grown comfortable in neutral—even if neutral is not God's best for us (and, P.S., it's not!).

Over the next six weeks, we are going to talk about some pretty weighty issues that can trip us up in the journey of faith. Some are issues that, at first glance, you will shrug off as not being a problem for you personally. Resist the temptation to skip a session. Many of us don't realize we're stuck because we've succumbed to a predictable, spiritual routine and learned to play the pretender game like seasoned professionals. I know this because I've been there. It wasn't until I took an honest appraisal of my heart that I realized I was a royal mess ... a gloriously, imperfect mess in need of a perfect and holy God. Being honest about where I was in the journey was liberating.

I suppose that's what I'm asking you to do in this study: be honest about where *you* are in the journey. In a nutshell, I'm asking you to *address the mess*.

So, what do you say? Do you want to stay where you are ... or get honest and move on?

Vicki Courtney

Cleanup on Aisle One!

You were born into a glorious mess,
and we all have become something of a glorious mess ourselves.
And in the midst of our mess, God has a thing for us. . . .
He is aware that we are but dust and our feet are made of clay,
and he has made arrangements for us to not stay that way.

STASI ELDREDGE

Welcome

Welcome to the first session of *Move On: When Mercy Meets Your Mess.* If you or any of your fellow group members do not know one another, take some time to introduce yourselves. Have each person share why she came to the small group and what she would like to take away from the experience by the end of the six weeks.

Video Teaching

As you watch the video for session one, use the following outline to record any thoughts or concepts that stand out to you.

We are all fellow sinners whose lives have been radically altered by God's grace.

Playing the "pretender" game will only leave us exhausted. What if we could be more honest about the challenges and struggles we all face in the Christian journey?

The truth is that each of us is a mess. Unfortunately, many Christians live out their days trying to pretend that their lives are not such muddy messes!

Most of us come to the realization that somewhere along the way, grace has shifted from being the solid foundation of our faith to a mere footnote in our belief system.

Has our once-vibrant faith devolved into familiar mediocrity? Are we simply going through the motions like a well-rehearsed dance number?

The heartbreaks and hurdles of life are meant to become trophies of God's grace rather than secrets to be buried.

It's easy to blend into the crowd and pretend all is well and good. However, if we want to be real, we must be willing to put up a fight.

Coming clean about our struggles and imperfections is like jumping off the back of a boat and trusting someone will catch us. But when we experience the mercy of God, staying on the boat and playing it safe is no longer an option.

Small Group Discussion

Take some time at this point to discuss with your fellow group members what you just watched and to explore these concepts in Scripture.

1. In the introduction to this session, I share about the time when my son told me his fiancée, Casey, was pregnant. When was a time you were confronted with something difficult that similarly changed the course of your life?

2. What fears did you have to face to be able to reveal that muddy mess to others? What response did you generally receive? How did that make you feel?

3. Describe a situation where you felt the unexpected grace of God through the actions of fellow believers. How did that experience encourage you to be more honest with yourself about your life?

4. **Read:** Romans 3:23. What does Paul remind us of in this verse? How does that apply to how you view—and even judge—other people?

5. **Read:** Psalm 51:6. What does this verse tell us God is after in regard to our heart attitude? How does this compel you to live authentically?

6. **Read:** Matthew 28:20b. "Jumping off the boat" and coming clean about our struggles can be a scary prospect. But what does Jesus promise in this verse? How does that truth give you strength to face your muddy messes?

Closing Prayer

Close your time together in prayer. Here are a few ideas on what you and your group members can pray based on the topic of this session:

○ Pray that God will give you boldness to face the messes in your life.

○ Pray that God will help you not to play the "pretender game."

○ Pray that God will enable you to be gracious to others.

○ Pray that God will give you the reassurance to know that He is always with you even in the midst of your muddy messes.

Recommended Reading

Review the preface, "The Mess that Changed Everything," and chapter 1, "Cleanup on Aisle One!" in the book *Move On: When Mercy Meets Your Mess.* If you have questions you want to bring to the next meeting, use the space provided below.

*For Ragamuffins, God's name is Mercy. We see our darkness
as a prized possession because it drives us into the heart of God.
Without mercy our darkness would plunge us into despair—
for some, self-destruction. Time alone with God reveals
the unfathomable depths of the poverty of the spirit.*

BRENNAN MANNING

Between-Sessions Personal Study

DAY 1: The Pretender Game

Pretending is a glorious part of growing up, one of the true joys of childhood. With no boundaries and no one telling us we can't do something, we are free to dream about our future. A scientist. A marine biologist. An astronaut. We can imagine ourselves in the long-lost city of Atlantis; rescue a puppy from a fire; create Camelot all over again. Castles. Submarines. Spaceships. The world is our playground.

When my kids were young, one of their all-time favorite toys was a foldout McDonald's drive-through food stand. It came complete with a cash register, an apron, and plastic imitations of just about every item offered on McDonald's menu. It even had a grill that, with a push of a button, could sizzle your pretend meat patty to plastic perfection. My kids logged more hours pretending in the drive-through food stand than I can count.

I knew it was getting a bit out of hand when a relative was visiting and asked my oldest son the familiar question, "Ryan, what do you want to be when you grow up?" Forget about the standard occupations that capture the attention of most preschool boys, like fireman or policeman. My son, without hesitation, answered, "I want to be a McDonald's worker person." That was my clue that maybe it was time to take a break from the food stand!

Pretending is liberating for a child. But if you carry the game into adulthood, it is soul-killing. The masks we wear suffocate us.

Can you relate?

Have you ever said "I'm fine," when inside you thought you would collapse with the weight of the shame you were bearing silently? Have you sat through an entire lunch with your friends, never revealing that you were seriously depressed and wondering if you'd be better off dead? Have you remained silent during prayer requests, making everybody think that all was well, while secretly you were reeling from the discovery that your husband was addicted to pornography? Or that you wanted out of your marriage altogether?

The Pretender Game isn't anything new. Our mothers played it. And their mothers. In fact, our spiritual ancestors were pretty good at it, too.

Read: 2 Samuel 11. You've probably read this story before, so if it's too familiar, try reading it in a different translation. As you read, don't focus on David's sin. Instead, pay attention to the actions David took to cover up his sin—to make sure nobody knew what was really going on in his life. Summarize the story in your own words.

What things did David do to hide his sin?

What words would you use to describe David in this story?

How are David's actions similar to yours? What have you done to make sure nobody knew you were hurting? Caught in sin?

David played the Pretender Game brilliantly. His cover-ups are the stuff of Lifetime movies. The king of Israel was supposed to be a religious leader as well as a political leader, but he failed both his people and his God. Only when confronted by the prophet Nathan (see 2 Samuel 12), did David come clean. After being disciplined by God, he famously penned the following words:

When I kept silent, my bones became brittle from my groaning all day long. For day and night Your hand was heavy on me; my strength was drained as in the summer's heat.

(Psalm 32:3–4 HCSB)

Pretense and denial had taken its toll. The phrase "my bones became brittle" comes from a Greek phrase that means "to waste away; to be consumed with cares."[1] How has the Pretender Game taken its toll on you? Your relationships with others? Your relationship with God? Take some time to jot down your thoughts.

While our masks feel comfortable, they wear us down. We waste away in a slow death behind the veneer of our plastic smiles. We will remain broken, wounded, and weary until we finally admit that the Pretender Game is killing us.

DAY 2: Perfectly Polished

As someone who has done women's events for many years, I've heard my fair share of confessions from hurting women. One in particular has been difficult to forget.

This woman approached me for prayer during a time of commitment at the end of the event, looking like she had stepped off a magazine cover. She was dressed fashionably from head to toe, her hair swept back in a neat ponytail, her makeup accentuating her radiant smile and beautiful eyes. Her figure was slender and toned, hinting that working out was a priority in her life. She was what the world would call "perfect."

And that was her problem. She wept on my shoulder as she confessed that she was exhausted from the pursuit of maintaining perfection. It certainly didn't help matters that her husband had insisted she see a personal trainer when her weight didn't come off as quickly as he wanted after giving birth to their last child. No wonder she was buckling under the pressure to be perfect! She was married to a selfish, insecure man whose approval was contingent on her outer appearance.

I prayed with her and strongly encouraged her to share her confession with a licensed counselor—and insist her husband come along with her. I've often wondered if she heeded my advice or fell back into her familiar routine of aiming for perfection. We've all felt pressures to conform to the world's formula for perfection, but this poor woman lived in that zip code 24/7. And the payoff? Nothing but misery.

Where does this intense pressure to be perfectly polished originate? The culprit—or at least a contributor—is our American culture.

We are assaulted with messages to be perfect every day. The perfect wife, the perfect soccer mom, the perfect cook, the perfect homemaker, the perfect party planner who must look gorgeously perfect while doing it all. Billboards. Commercials. Pinterest. Movies. TV shows (when will they show a normal family?). Even ads on the games you play on your smart phone. A dozen times a day—at least—you are reminded that you need to do more, be more, try more.

Take outward appearance as an obvious example. In 2012, an estimated 14.6 million people underwent plastic surgery,[2] to the tune of more than $11 billion.[3] Yes. *Billion*. We spent an additional $20 billion on weight-loss products, including diet books, diet drugs, and weight-loss surgeries.[4] Together, that money could wipe out global hunger in a matter of a decade.[5] Do you see the irony?

Clearly, our culture has taught us that it's not okay to be imperfect.

Our drive for perfection is certainly not confined to the body. We want our children to bring home straight *A*s from teachers and admiration from their peers. Our husbands need to wear the best title and claim the corner office. Houses immaculate. Yards pristine. Classroom snacks creative and unique. Smiles on, unwavering, even when an atomic bomb has exploded within. Anything less is ... well, unacceptable.

Does Scripture speak to our propensity to focus on perfection? Of having everything together? Of being the best soccer mom/entrepreneur/lover/homework-solver/friend/Christian?

Read: 1 Samuel 16:7 and Luke 16:14–15. What do these two passages have in common?

How do you try to "justify yourself in the eyes of others"?

What do people highly value in today's culture?

In your community?

In your church?

If God were to look in your heart, what would it tell Him about your drive to present yourself as polished and "all together"?

Throughout Scripture, God reminds us that what matters is what lies within the heart, not how we window-dress:

For the eyes of the LORD run to and fro throughout the whole earth, to show Himself strong on behalf of those whose heart is loyal to Him.

(2 CHRONICLES 16:9 NKJV)

May these words of my mouth and this meditation of my heart be pleasing in your sight, LORD, my Rock and my Redeemer.

(PSALM 19:14)

Above all else, guard your heart, for it is the wellspring of life.

(PROVERBS 4:23 NIV 1984)

For where your treasure is, there your heart will be also.

(MATTHEW 6:21)

The world's values—including the exaltation of outward appearances— are diametrically opposed to God's values. If we are not careful, we will allow that value system to creep into our thoughts, become embedded in our attitudes, and show itself in the way we act. Our culture's values are insidious because of their stealth-like nature. You won't hear a PSA announcement on TV warning about the damaging effects of living by today's culture. There's no nonprofit chartered to expose it. Unfortunately, you only see its effects when the damage is done—divorce, bankruptcy, suicide, eating disorders, anxiety. I'm not saying that all of those stem from the pursuit of polished perfection, but I do think it's a factor.

To close today's Bible study, ask God to reveal the condition of your heart. Ask yourself:

○ Is my heart loyal to Him, or am I more loyal to my reputation among my peers?

○ If God examined the meditation of my heart, what would He see as the focus of my life? Looking good in front of others? Making sure no one sees what lies beneath? Hiding my true self?

○ Have I guarded myself against the world's pursuit of perfection?

○ What do I treasure in my heart?

These questions may be painful, but if you want mercy to meet you in your mess, you must be willing to own it.

DAY 3: **The Root of the Problem**

Kudzu.

In some places, it's called the Mile-a-minute Vine. Foot-a-night Vine. Miracle Vine. Porch Vine. Telephone Vine. The Wonder Vine. In the lower parts of the U.S., it is known as "The Vine that Ate the South."

If you've traveled below the Mason-Dixon Line, especially to the Deep South, you've likely seen this hearty little plant covering everything—trees, road signs, buildings, and even junkyard cars. Most visitors comment on its beautiful, lush, green color. Those who live in the South curse its very existence.

Why? Because you can't kill kudzu (well, you can eventually over multiple seasons and a gazillion chemicals, but that requires a long, scientific explanation). It's a battle you (almost) never win. Its tap root is massive: 7 inches in diameter (at least), 6 feet in length, and weighing up to 400 pounds. One single root crown can produce as many as 30 vines.[6] It can reach up to 60 feet in height.[7] Its vines can grow a full foot in one day and over 60 feet in a season.[8] The weight of the vines can bring down power lines and collapse buildings.[9]

Here's the most interesting and pertinent fact about kudzu. It kills everything agricultural in its path—trees, grass, shrubs, and other plants. It covers other plants and blocks out the sunlight until the vegetation dies. Trees even collapse under its weight.

Why would I mention this plant trivia? Because it makes a great illustration of what pretending can do. Playing games, wearing masks, hiding behind the veneer of a plastic smile, whitewashing your struggles, and sanitizing your sin—all of it is kudzu to your soul. When pretending takes root into your life, it will cover and destroy everything in its path—your worldview, your outlook, your relationships, your future, and especially your relationship with God. Over time, you will collapse under the weight of what you hide.

Read: Psalm 38:1–8. Describe the emotional tone of these verses.

Underline all of the words and phrases David used to describe his spiritual state. Circle the descriptors you have experienced because you hid your weaknesses, failures, and sin from others:

Pierced	Angry	Humiliated	Forsaken
Overwhelmed	Sad	Hateful	Burdened
Weakened	Failure	Bowed down	Ashamed
Troubled	Low	Lonely	Feeble
Vengeful	Crushed	Repentant	Unhealthy
Frustrated	Mourning		

What did David say was the reason for his troubled state?

David painted an apt but dismal portrayal of a life buried under the weight of unconfessed sin—what we call pretending. You've probably experienced similar emotions as well, because no one can bear the load of living a "perfect" life. You may be able to wear your mask for a while, but over time, it will drain the life from you and leave you for dead. You will end up weak, overwhelmed, crushed, and burdened. Collapse is imminent.

Jesus said that He came to give us life abundant (John 10:10b), but many of us have mistakenly concluded that Jesus was just talking about heaven and that life here is simply a matter of survival. Hunker down for now and wait until the roll is called up yonder. To bide our time until eternity, we trade in a life of authenticity and honesty (which is way too scary) and bury ourselves in our kids' successes, our manicured nails and fad diets, and a thousand other unhealthy escapes. All the while, abundant life escapes our grasp, and we are left wanting for something more.

How has pretending that everything is "just fine" damaged your life? How has pretending crushed your spirit? Take some time to complete the following sentence starters prayerfully and thoughtfully.

Unconfessed sin has caused problems in my relationships (friends, family, spouse, children) by:

Pretending that everything is under control has left me with:

The thought of being honest about my sin and weaknesses causes me to feel:

Playing a role I've created instead of being real with others has:

I'd love to be able to tell someone that:

If only people knew that:

Fortunately, your story doesn't have to end there. God always provides a way out. **Read:** Proverbs 28:13. What is God's solution?

We'll learn more about that solution tomorrow, but for now, ask yourself, why will God not allow someone who conceals sin to prosper?

DAY 4: All-y All-y in Come Free

While recently babysitting my two-year-old grandson, I gave him the familiar five-minute warning that his parents were on their way to pick him up. He didn't much care for the news, given that Mimi and Pop's house has few rules and no limits to the amount of miniature Reese's peanut butter cups one can consume in a single visit. I have to give him props for what he did next. "Mimi, hurry ... hide." Yep, he wanted to hide from his mom and dad.

He chose his favorite (and predictable) spot, which was behind the sofa in our game room. As an extra measure, he wanted me to drape the throw over our heads. When his mom and dad arrived at the house, the familiar game began. Operation I'm-not-going-home was underway. His parents were troopers and played along for several minutes. "Where are Walker and Mimi? I wonder where they could be this time?"

Finally, his daddy lifted the blanket from over our heads and the gig was up. Again. Until the next visit.

Hide-and-seek. It's not just a game kids play. Adults have mastered it, too. Can you think of a hide-and-seek game in the Bible? Believe it or not, there is one—in the very first book. Remember it now?

> When the woman saw that the fruit of the tree was good for food and pleasing to the eye, and also desirable for gaining wisdom, she took some and ate it. She also gave some to her husband, who was with her, and he ate it. Then the eyes of both of them were opened, and they realized they were naked; so they sewed fig leaves together and made coverings for themselves. Then the man and his wife heard the sound of the Lord God as he was walking in the garden in the cool of the day, and they hid from the Lord God among the trees of the garden. But the Lord God called to the man, "Where are you?" He answered, "I heard you in the garden, and I was afraid because I was naked; so I hid." (Genesis 3:6–10)

The first hiding game took place between the Creator and his creation. Adam and Eve became conscious of their sin, and it left them feeling afraid, ashamed, and naked before God (no pun intended). Just like many of us, they tried to hide from God. They staked out a spot in the middle of the trees and hoped that God wouldn't find them as He was walking in the garden. If you're tempted to laugh at them for such ludicrous behavior—who can hide from God, right?—think about your own attempts to hide.

> *I'll join that Bible study, so people won't know I'm struggling.*
>
> *I'll help my kid with his homework, so nobody will know he's not a great student.*
>
> *I'll keep busy with so many activities that I won't have time to sit still before God.*
>
> *I'll hide my depression by cracking jokes and helping others laugh.*

I know. I've been there. I can spot a game of hide-and-seek at twenty paces. If you're like me, you don't even realize that you're playing the game. Hiding and pretending is second nature to you, like brushing your teeth or using the turn signal. Sometimes wearing a veneer seems like the only way to navigate a painful situation.

Isn't that what Adam and Eve were doing? Scripture says they were afraid of God. Why? Because they had betrayed Him, forsaken His offers of abundant life and love eternal. They had rebelled against their Creator, so they expected a response from Him—a response that would no doubt bring pain. Avoiding pain is the most logical thing to do, right?

Fortunately, God knew better. He wouldn't allow Adam and Eve to stay hidden for long. He went looking for them, remember (see verses 8–9)? He could have waited. He could have stayed on His heavenly throne and let the First Family experience a life of misery from hidden sin and broken relationship. He could have scrapped them and started over with a new couple. However, God does just the opposite. He brings the hidden out into the open.

Why? Because that's the only way to find freedom.

The only way you and I will ever find freedom is to come out into the open. Take off our masks. Believe that it's okay NOT to be okay. Admit our sin. Come clean about our weaknesses, fears, temptations, and struggles. Until then, we bear the weight of our sin and shame, our failures and our flimsy faith.

Remember the story of David and how he tried to cover up? His story doesn't end there. If you read on, David confesses his sin. He receives God's discipline, but it was better than hiding in guilt. The psalm he wrote in conjunction with this story tells us so.

Read: Psalm 51:1 – 17. Describe the emotional tone in David's confession.

List all of the phrases that describe what David wanted from God.

Have you ever been this brutally honest with God about your life? Have you ever laid it all before Him, hiding nothing and exposing everything? Describe that experience.

Have you ever benefited from hiding from God and others?

In this beautiful poem to God, David reminds all of us that coming clean before God is worth the cost. Being honest is the only path to wholeness. Living transparently before God and before others guards us against the trap of perfection and performance, and it offers us the chance to receive and give grace. Otherwise, we run from tree to tree, playing hide-and-seek with the rest of the world, and after a while, that game just isn't fun anymore.

DAY 5: **No Polished Patriarchs**

"My sweet husband sent me flowers today for no reason!"

"Headed out for a two-mile run!"

"My daughter just tried out for the volleyball team and made the first cut!"

Social networking sites can offer a sneak peek into our friends' lives, but the sneak peek often amounts to nothing more than a highlight reel. Rarely do we see a family picture where the teenager is sporting the classic surly expression. Or the status update asking for prayers for a crumbling marriage. Or the snapshot of the family garage that looks like it could qualify for an episode on *Hoarders* (busted!). Not that I'm endorsing that level of TMI, but it would be nice to see a little less pretending and a lot more honesty.

I am glad that the Bible doesn't give us sanitized versions of the lives of the predecessors of our faith. Instead, Scripture has left for us the honest confessions of people who, rather than glossing over their struggles with a weak copy of real spirituality, openly admitted their failures, temptations, and most importantly, their authentic relationship with God.

Read: Job 3:11–17, 24–26. Summarize Job's honest monologue. What does he long for?

What conclusions does he make?

If Job lived today and he voiced his heart in your Bible study group, how do you think people would respond?

In much of the book, Job asks God about his plight. He is full of questions, yet he never accuses God. What is the difference between asking and accusing?

I love Job because he didn't spout meaningless dribble when he sat in those ashes. He didn't remind himself that what doesn't kill you makes you stronger. He didn't make excuses for why God had allowed his devastating calamity. Instead, he voiced an honest desire to see the face of God. And in the end, God honored his request.

Another character in the Old Testament was blatantly honest about his life. At first glance, you might not think of him as a role model for coming clean and moving on. Read more carefully, and you'll see his honesty.

Read: Ecclesiastes 1:1 – 11. Record everything you know about Solomon and about the message of Ecclesiastes.

How would you describe Solomon's attitude in these opening verses? What do you know about him that would support your description?

Solomon became king after his father David died. In addition to being wiser than any person before or since him (1 Kings 3:12), he was also an honest seeker who wanted to find meaning in his life. He sought it out in wisdom, pleasure, and wealth, all to no avail. Nothing brought lasting happiness. (In the end, though, he acknowledges his need for God.)

Our culture is teeming with people trying to find meaning in the same places as Solomon—education, wealth, status, pleasure, and gluttony. But unlike Solomon, most people (including Christians) would never admit that while their lifestyles may seem enviable to others, inwardly they are dying. Rather than risk their pride, they buy another boat, earn another degree, teach another class, drink another glass of wine. Solomon was wise enough to know the freeing power of honesty and authenticity.

Hands down, the best example of authenticity comes from Paul, former murderer of Christians turned missionary/evangelist. Despite writing thirteen books of the New Testament, he held no false image of himself, nor did he try to portray one in his letters to the churches.

Read: Romans 7:15 – 25. Rewrite these verses in your own words.

How have you experienced a similar struggle with sin? Be specific.

What does Paul call himself at the end of his confession? Why do you think he used that description? Have you ever felt that way?

Let's take off our church masks for a moment and admit that all of us have felt the same way. I want to refrain from gossip, but before I know it, I'm dishing out the latest dirt with a girlfriend. I want to respond in love to people who are different from me, but I still cross the street and hold my purse a little tighter when I see a homeless man. I deeply long to live in authenticity and transparency, but I find myself putting on my fake smile more often than I'd like. I know you do, too.

Just like Solomon and Job, Paul found liberation in being honest before God and others. And you, too, can find that same liberation if you're willing to take the risk. So join me in that journey as we move on to the place where mercy meets us in the midst of our mess.

Move On Challenge

Write a letter to God, either in the space provided below or on a separate sheet of paper. Be honest and tell Him how you feel about yourself, your family, and your church. Even if you are in a chapter where you are angry or cynical—tell Him. Don't censor yourself. This is the first and most critical step in finding healing from the mistakes and wounds you've hidden for far too long.

Unclaimed Baggage

*Just when we think we've messed up so badly that our lives
are nothing but heaps of ashes, God pours His living water over us
and mixes the ashes into clay. He then takes this clay and molds it
into a vessel of beauty. After He fills us with His overflowing love,
He can use us to pour His love into the hurting lives of others.*

LYSA TERKEURST

Welcome

Welcome to session two of *Move On: When Mercy Meets Your Mess*. Before watching the video, briefly discuss with each other what has been happening in your lives during the week. Also discuss any key points that stood out to you from the between-sessions personal study and any questions that came up since the last session.

Video Teaching

As you watch the video for session two, use the following outline to record any thoughts or concepts that stand out to you.

As believers, we accepted God's grace and forgiveness when we came to Christ. We became a new creation and eligible for an "upgrade." So why do we still cling to our former identities and try to troubleshoot the issues that arise from carrying the shame of our past into our new lives?

Christ has set us free, but many of us refuse to let the old pass away. We may even feel pressured by our fellow believers to continue hiding our secret sin. However, we can know that God will meet us every step of the way when we surrender to Him.

Jesus didn't initiate the conversation with the Samaritan woman because He wanted water from the well to quench His physical thirst. Rather, He wanted to offer her living water to quench her spiritual thirst.

Jesus did not call out the Samaritan woman to harass or shame her but rather to show her how desperately she needed what He was offering. He knew that living water would be of no value to her unless she was first willing to acknowledge her mess.

A true encounter with God's mercy will take us from the depths of despair and leave us wanting to shout from the rooftops. As our shame is lifted away by Christ's nail-scarred hands of love, we are able to direct others to God's mercy.

On the cross, Jesus cried out, "It is finished" (John 19:30). To doubt God's forgiveness, in a sense, is to add a footnote with a list of exceptions to His declaration.

Healing comes when we learn to "neglect" an accuser's shameful reminders of our past sins. In doing so, shame loses the power to control our lives.

Mercy is always willing to meet us in our mess. So why do we often try to clean up our messes in our own power — or ignore them altogether?

Small Group Discussion

Take some time at this point to discuss with your fellow group members what you just watched and to explore these concepts in Scripture.

1. In the introduction to this session, I share about how my husband was eligible for an upgrade to his smart phone but chose to keep his old, familiar, lake-drenched model. In what ways are you still holding onto the "unclaimed baggage" of your past sins? How are you allowing those sins to define you?

2. **Read:** John 4:1–30. What shame was the Samaritan woman hiding? Why did Jesus tell her to go and call her husband if He already knew her story?

3. What did Jesus mean when He told the woman that He would give her "living water"? Why do those who drink from this water never thirst again?

4. What were the results of the woman's encounter with Christ? What have been the results in your life after your encounter with Christ?

5. How have the harsh and judgmental words spoken over you affected your ability to let go of your messes? How have you, perhaps like the Samaritan woman, felt pressured to continue hiding your sins and play the "pretender game"?

6. In what ways has Christ offered you His living water and met you in the midst of your mess? How has He released you from the past and lifted your shame and despair?

Closing Prayer

Close your time together in prayer. Here are a few ideas on what you and your group members can pray based on the topic of this session:

○ Pray that God will help you let go of your past shame.

○ Pray that you will truly know "it is finished" and Christ has set you free.

○ Pray that God will help you forgive those who have spoken judgmental and condescending words to you in the past.

○ Pray that God will meet you in your mess and give you healing.

Recommended Reading

Review chapter 4, "Unclaimed Baggage," in *Move On: When Mercy Meets Your Mess.* If you have questions you want to bring to the next meeting, use the space provided below.

"It is finished!" Every stumbling block is rolled out of the road;
every gate is opened; the bars of brass are broken;
the gates of iron are burst asunder.
"It is finished!" Come and be welcome!

CHARLES SPURGEON

Between-Sessions Personal Study

DAY 1: A Closer Look

One of the biggest curses related to aging is the inability to read the small print on labels absent a pair of readers. I finally broke down and bought an extra pair to have on hand in the kitchen after burning a frozen lunch to an inedible crisp in my microwave one afternoon. The heating instructions were a blur and apparently I mistook the "3" for an "8" and as a result, my happy home reeked of burnt tomato sauce for weeks. But that was the least of my worries. After cleaning the charred remains from the inner chamber of my microwave, I concluded it would have been easier to purchase a new one. Had I just grabbed my readers and taken a closer look at the instructions, I could have avoided the Lean Cuisine explosion.

On a much deeper level, many of us have a blurry understanding of shame and guilt, often mistaking one for the other. When we fail to examine the difference between the two words, we can mistakenly assume that God administers a brand of guilt that leads to shame. This faulty thinking can lead to untold amounts of damage over the years. Today, we are going to take a closer look at these two words and begin to clean up the mess.

Read: Psalm 32:1–7. Describe the tone of this psalm.

Which is illustrated here—guilt or shame? How do you know? List the words and phrases that help you come to your conclusion.

I seriously doubt that David would have considered God a hiding place if he felt shame in His presence. He would feel God's disapproval, not His protection. And David certainly wouldn't have written, "You surround me with joyful shouts of deliverance" (HCSB) if he thought God was out to squash him like an irritating ant. This psalm is an expression of a fallible, sinful man who had experienced the forgiveness and restoration of the Lord.

Read: Psalm 103:8–12. In the left column, list all the words and phrases that describe God's character. In the right column, list the words and phrases that describe God's actions toward His people (that's you and me).

God's Character	God's Actions

Why would I have you create this list? Because I wanted you to see that God's character motivates His responses toward us. It is because of His compassion and grace that He will not always (continually) accuse us. Because of His faithful love, He has separated us from our sin. He didn't want our sin to define us, accuse us, or paralyze us. Shame would never offer that freedom. Shame ties us to our sin and our past. Unfortunately, that's not the only thing shame does. The chart on the next page describes the characteristics of both guilt (conviction of sin) and shame. Hopefully, it will give more clarity about their differences.

Guilt	Shame
"I did something wrong."	"I am wrong."
Convicts	Condemns
Leads to change (repentance)	Leads to resignation and helplessness
Results in restoration	Results in isolation
Passes over time	Stays and deepens over time
Frees a person	Enslaves a person
Takes responsibility	Blames others
Discipline	Punishment

See the difference? Guilt affirms. Shame destroys.

Let me be very clear: Shame is not from God. Shame comes from the pit of hell and is orchestrated by an enemy who wants to destroy you (John 10:10a). He will use whatever means necessary—including your past mistakes—to make sure you do not experience the abundant life Jesus promised (John 10:10b). God uses the conviction of the Holy Spirit to draw you back to Himself. Satan uses shame to make sure you hide from God. Isn't that what happened in the Garden? It was shame that drove Adam and Eve to hide from God. However, God sought out our ancestral parents to bring restoration.

And He offers the same to us.

DAY 2: We the Jury . . .

I recently read about a Texas judge who handed out an unusual sentence to a convicted drunk driver. The driver had killed a man while driving under the influence, and he was ordered to stand at the scene of the crash for the next four Saturdays from 9 a.m. to 5 p.m. while wearing a sign admitting to his guilt. The judge also required the defendant to keep a picture of the crash in his living room as part of the punishment, and probation officers would visit the crash site and conduct random home visits to ensure the orders were followed. Apparently, this was the man's second DUI, and the judge must have felt that his selfish and sinful choices would continue to put innocent others into harm's way unless the defendant felt the sting of shame. Some commended the judge for the sentence, while others felt it was barbaric.

Fortunately, God, our great Judge, is much kinder and doesn't require us to carry around signs advertising our sins and shortcomings. Jesus lugged our sins up Calvary's hill and nailed each one to the cross. Yet, some Christians can't seem to leave them there. The sentence has been handed down, but we continue to play judge and jury—condemning, judging, and pronouncing penalty—on ourselves.

Most of the time, we're not aware of what we're doing. It's as natural as taking the next breath or blinking in the bright sunlight. The condemnation comes as a voice that whispers to us in the quiet moments when no one else is around. Every time we argue with our husband or lose our tempers with our kids. When we look in the mirror or step on the scale. When we make an impulse purchase. When we flashback to a past sin.

Can you recognize the judgments?

"That was so stupid! How could you say that?"

"You look awful!"

"You will never measure up to _____."

"Why would your husband love you?"

"If you were a better mother, you wouldn't yell."

"You can't do anything right."

"They wouldn't love you if they knew about _____"
   (something in your past).

"A real Christian wouldn't _____" (choose a sin).

"You're a loser."

Perhaps Paul experienced his share of shame. After all, in his pre-Christian days, he had sent Christians to their deaths. Maybe because of his own rounds with judgment, the Holy Spirit led him to pen Romans 8:1–11. **Read** the passage now. Why is there no condemnation for believers?

From what has the Spirit set you free personally?

According to this passage, use the following chart to list the differences between life in the flesh and life in the Spirit.

Life in the Flesh	Life in the Spirit

What does the Holy Spirit give you? (v. 10) What is the reason for that life? (v. 10)

What does it mean to be made righteous before God?

There is NO condemnation for believers. NONE. In the original Greek, the word "condemnation" is used in reference to divine judgment against sin.[10] Think of it as a legal term by which God pronounces a sentence in light of the sin committed against Him. In other words, because of Christ, God does not pronounce us guilty and then punish us. We are declared "not guilty." That's amazing news.

But it gets better. The phrase "there is now" is used to refer to something done in the present time.[11] Present moment. Right now. You. Me. Forgiven. At. This very instant. No matter the sin, there is no condemnation. None. Ever. Because Jesus suffered God's judgment on the cross, you don't. You are forgiven. Nothing you do takes away your right standing before God because *you* didn't earn that right standing. Jesus provided it. And God declared it. Forever. God is the only rightful Judge and He has already declared you innocent.

When you feel trapped by the shame of your past sins, you are not experiencing God's conviction. God doesn't shame His beloved. Rather, you are buying into the lies of the Father of Lies (John 8:44) who specializes in dishing out shame. This passage tells us that God offers life and peace (Romans 8:6, 10). And living under the weight of shame certainly isn't peaceful or life-giving. Shame lurks in the shadows, slowly and methodically draining the life and joy and peace and hope that are yours.

The question is simple: Do you want to live in the freedom of forgiveness offered to you through Christ, or do you want to remain ensnared by shame perpetuated by Satan?

The choice is yours.

DAY 3: **What's the Catch?**

We've all heard the saying, "If it sounds too good to be true, it probably is." I was reminded of this wisdom recently when I saw an ad for one of my favorite department stores touting a "storewide sale." I had had my eye on a leather handbag at the store for several months and had been waiting for it to go on sale. When I arrived at the store and took the treasured bag to the checkout, the sales clerk rang it up as full price. When I showed her the ad advertising the "storewide" discount, she showed me the tiny fine print at the bottom that listed a dozen or more "excluded brands" from the sale. Ugh. I put the bag back and left the store frustrated that the "storewide sale" had a catch.

When it comes to God's offer of forgiveness, it's easy to assume there must be a catch. Surely, there's something in the fine print that details a few biggie sins that aren't covered in His offer, right? Wrong. Why then, do many of us carry shame and punish ourselves if the penalty has been paid in full?

Read: John 19:28–30. Verse 28 says that "everything was now accomplished" (HCSB). What exactly had been accomplished?

Why do you think Jesus chose that particular moment to fulfill the Scripture about His thirst (Psalm 69:21)? Why not ask for it earlier in the crucifixion?

What are the final words of Jesus in these verses?

Picture that scene at the foot of the cross, and describe the emotion(s) you sense as Jesus declared those final words.

Our familiarity with the events that took place on the day of Jesus' death can sometimes numb us to significant nuances. For instance, we know that asking for the wine fulfilled a prophecy. But why would Jesus choose that moment to ask for the numbing drink? Why not ask for it at the height of the pain and suffering? Why drink it right before death? While Scripture does not specifically tell us, we can infer a possibility based on what happened next—His final words. Jesus needed to wet His parched lips and dry throat in order to pronounce some of the most important words in Scripture:

It. Is. Finished.

Addiction? It is finished.

Adultery? It is finished.

Lust? It is finished.

A negative spirit? It is finished.

A hard heart? It is finished.

In those three words, Jesus proclaimed that the work of redemption was complete. Done. Nothing else was needed. Especially not shame. He bore that on the cross too (Hebrews 12:2). The work of buying you back with His blood was complete. His last words were a cry of victory and a declaration of your liberation.

Still think you must somehow bear your shame? That you bring it on yourself because you keep messing up? **Read:** Hebrews 12:1–2. What does it say about shame?

Jesus bore our shame so that we wouldn't need to. He carried that weight away with every lash of the whip and every drop of blood that dropped to the ground. When Jesus endured the cross and despised the shame, He opened the door for us to come boldly before the throne of grace (Hebrews 4:16), free of shame and confident before Him.

Shame tells us that we are not worthy. The cross tells us we are.

Shame tells us we are despised by God and others. The cross tells us we are God's beloved.

Shame drives us away from the cross. The cross drives away shame and strips it of its power.

The problem is that you and I empower shame. Every time we make an agreement with the enemy about our inadequacies, we fuel it a little bit more. Each time we believe a lie, we give the enemy more space in the corners of our heart until it takes over.

So how do we break free?

By refusing to believe the lies.

By kicking shame to the curb when it tries to make itself at home.

By reminding yourself that when Jesus died on that cross, He bore your shame. And He destroyed its power.

I want to ask you to do something very bold. List below any sin that weighs you down with shame.

Now, I want you to write beside each sin above, "It is finished."

Every time you hear those whispers of shame in the back of your head, simply ask yourself one question: Is this from God? If not, then replace that thought with the truth.

You are loved. You are forgiven. You are God's beloved. It is finished.

That alone defines you.

DAY 4: **Shame, the Verb**

We've all experienced the sting of hurtful words that bring shame. I remember when my oldest son was four years old and I had signed him up for swim lessons with a woman who was rumored to be the best of the best. She taught the lessons in her backyard pool and her summer classes filled up quickly. I was thrilled when she called to let me know there was one spot left in one of her weeklong classes. The classes went well and I enjoyed visiting with the other mothers by the poolside while our children were learning the basics.

On the last day of class, we were all saying our goodbyes by the pool as we gathered up our belongings. Noticing that my son was heading out the backyard gate without his towel, I said, "Ryan, can you come get your towel, please?" And that's when I received a heavy dose of shaming from his swim instructor who quickly reprimanded me in front of the other mothers. "Why are you *asking* him to get his towel? It shouldn't be *his* choice, now should it? He's more likely to respect you as his mother if you tell him to mind you rather than ask him to mind you." Ouch. There was an awkward silence as my face flushed with embarrassment. One of the other mothers lightened the moment by mumbling under her breath as we exited the backyard, "Wow, maybe the bigger crime is having a mother who's as cranky and bossy as she is." We all laughed, but I've never forgotten the sting of shame I felt over the instructor's condemning words.

Shame is a noun, but it can also be a verb. We can shame others. Show them disgrace and dishonor them. Discredit, degrade, and debase them. Humiliate them. Take them down a peg or two, cut them down to size. And oftentimes, we take pleasure in it. We are always so eager to point out the sin of others, as if we had none of our own.

One of the most tender and intimate moments in Jesus' ministry takes place against the backdrop of shame. You've probably read it before, but I want to reexamine it from a different perspective.

Read: John 8:1–11. Rather than putting yourself in the woman's place, identifying with her shame and disgrace, I want you to immerse yourself in the story as if you were one of the teachers of the law, one of the Pharisees. In the space provided below, write a monologue to describe the event. Use all of your senses—sight, touch, hearing, taste, smell.

What was it like for you to play the role of the Pharisee?

Nobody likes the Pharisees. You won't see a book on the Christian best-seller list that outlines the five secrets of being a religious hypocrite. You're not likely to hear a sermon challenging you to follow their example. You certainly don't want to be described as one. Unfortunately, all of us are guilty of playing that role from time to time.

Take an honest look at some of the following sentences. Note the ones that you've said out loud—or inside your head.

"I can't believe she wore that."

"I knew she wasn't as perfect as she seemed."

"Our pastor just isn't doing the job. That's why nobody comes anymore."

"Those kids are out of control. I'm glad my kids don't _____."

"She is such a snob. No wonder nobody likes her."

"She lets her kids listen to that music. I would never let mine hear that garbage."

"I'm glad my husband doesn't _____."

"I bet she's had plastic surgery. Nobody can look that good naturally."

When we shame people, we act as prosecutor, judge, and jury. Like the religious leaders in today's gospel story, we "tie up heavy loads that are hard to carry and put them on people's shoulders, but [we] ... aren't willing to lift a finger to move them" (Matthew 23:4 HCSB). And if some of us are honest, we'd admit that we like to do things for other people in order to be seen; we love the place of honor at church. We love to be treated with respect and lauded for our amazing Christian walk (Matthew 23:5–7).

We are more like those Pharisees than we'd like to admit.

The only antidote to shaming others is to return to Golgotha. Look up at the cross and recognize that He bore your sins, too. Look around. Notice the other people, also at the feet of the Savior. Recognize that we're all equal at the foot of the cross. It is the great leveling ground. No matter your economic background or religious heritage, regardless of your past sin or future accomplishments, everything fades into the background as the love of God takes the spotlight. We stand—together and alone—in need of redemption.

> *On a hill far away stood an old rugged cross,*
> *The emblem of suffering and shame;*
> *And I love that old cross where the dearest and best*
> *For a world of lost sinners was slain.*

DAY 5: **Repurposed for a Purpose**

About fifteen years ago, I was visiting an aunt whom I rarely see and she handed me a box as I was leaving. In the box were several old antique doll-house dolls that had been passed down to her from her late husband's family. She mentioned that they were very old and that one of them, a tiny three-inch wood peg doll, dated back to the early 1800s. I graciously thanked her for the kind gift and, upon arriving home, tucked the box onto a top shelf in my closet and forgot all about the poor dolls.

Recently, I stumbled upon the box and vaguely recalled my aunt giving me the dolls. As I pulled each one out of the tissue wrap that had protected them, I found the tiny wood peg doll. I've since gained an appreciation for antique treasures that offer a glimpse into an era long-forgotten, so I was curious to find out a bit more about her. She looked to be wearing her original clothes and her wooded arms and legs were still attached. Her face was hand-painted and she also had boots that were painted red. I was able to locate a doll appraiser online who, much to my shock, informed me that the little doll dated back to approximately 1820–1850 and was highly desired among antique doll collectors with a worth estimated between $1,500–2,000! And to think, she had been sitting on a shelf for over a decade, forgotten, and gathering dust. Today, she lives in a small shadow box that is proudly displayed in my home.

Perhaps you can relate to that wood peg doll. You have a story, but you often feel invisible and forgotten. Or maybe, you feel like your story is not as significant as others' stories. Or maybe, you've resigned yourself to the shelf—refusing to believe God would ever use you as part of His kingdom agenda.

As Christians, it's easy to feel that way sometimes when we compare ourselves to others who seem to have a bigger role in God's story. Yet every story, every life, is of equal importance to God. God is in the business of making old things new, but many of us are still clinging to the old.

> Therefore, if anyone is in Christ, the new creation has come: The old has gone, the new is here! All this is from God, who reconciled us to himself through Christ and gave us the ministry of reconciliation.
>
> (2 Corinthians 5:17–18)

Did you catch that? When God saved you and made you new, He also gave you a new mission: the ministry of reconciliation. Or, as the Contemporary English Version paraphrases, "making peace between himself [God] and others." Like one beggar telling another beggar where to find bread, we are charged with the task of leading others to the Source of Life we have found.

I know what some of you are thinking: "That applies to other people, not me." Believe me, I've bought into that lie myself a time or two (or three or four). It sounds something like this:

"My mistakes are too great."

"My past is too horrendous."

"No one would believe me anyway."

"My family would laugh."

"I don't have what it takes."

"I'm not smart enough."

"I'm no Mother Teresa."

You're right. You are not Mother Teresa. You are you. The person God designed you to be. And when He saved you and re-created you, He did so with purpose.

Read: 1 Peter 2:9–12. Read it in several translations if you can. List all of the words and phrases that describe who you are:

List all of the words and phrases that describe what God wants you to do:

What do these verses tell you about God's plan for you?

These verses say nothing about sitting on the shelf, the sideline, or the bench. These verses are a call to action because of your new identity in Christ.

You are chosen.

Holy.

Royalty.

You are a priest.

His possession.

Mercy recipient and mercy bearer.

Praise proclaimer.

Light bearer.

Yes, you are a trophy of God's grace, but not like those that line the shelves in a trophy case. You are a living trophy of grace. Your everyday, going-to-work-again, non-journey-to-Africa life is a daily testimony of the relentless and redemptive love of God. The way you live and work and fight and drive and buy groceries and eat lunch and go to the movies—all of it is a story unfolding for others to see. It's a story of the God of heaven who loves and redeems. It's a story of what God does with a life surrendered to Him in the big things and the small. It's a story of betrayal and forgiveness, loss and redemption, death and new life.

You are repurposed for a purpose.

Go and live it out. Now.

Move On Challenge

Find some time this week to go before God and reflect on the moment (or moments) when mercy intersected with your mess. What's your story? Tell God you are ready for Him to repurpose your past. Take a minute to jot down three to five ways your story can be repurposed and used for His glory.

Us and Them

Do not waste time bothering whether you "love" your neighbor;
act as if you did. As soon as you do this you find one
of the great secrets: when you are behaving as if you loved someone,
you will presently come to love him.

C. S. LEWIS

Welcome

Welcome to session three of *Move On: When Mercy Meets Your Mess*. Before watching the video, briefly discuss with each other what has been happening in your lives during the week. Also discuss any key points that stood out to you from the between-sessions personal study and any questions that came up since the last session.

Video Teaching

As you watch the video for session three, use the following outline to record any thoughts or concepts that stand out to you.

Common ground can be found when two opposing forces put down their "weapons" and focus on their similarities rather than their differences.

When we start to see people for who they truly are, we may be shocked to find that the other side — the "them" group — does things in line with our values and beliefs.

We will become more aware of our similarities with the "them" group when we stand *with them* rather than *across from them*.

An act of love is generally more effective in sharing the message of Christ than serving up a litany of Bible verses or engaging in theological discussions.

When we cross the invisible dividing line separating "us" and "them," we experience the blessing of talking *with* other groups rather than *about* those groups.

Jesus led by example when it comes to closing the gap between "us" and "them." He was no stranger to the outcasts and the "least of these" (Matthew 25:40). In fact, He preferred the "them" crowd to the "us" crowd on the majority of days.

Jesus is our ultimate role model when it comes to extending genuine kindness to others. What if we were to follow His lead from this point forward?

Who is on our personal "them" list? What would it take for us to do away with our notions of "us" and "them" and begin to see ourselves as part of a collective "we"?

Small Group Discussion

Take some time at this point to discuss with your fellow group members what you just watched and to explore these concepts in Scripture.

1. In the introduction to this session, I share a story about the Christmas truce between British and German soldiers during World War I. What surprised you when you heard the story? What does this tell you about our ability to find common ground?

2. Have you ever found yourself in a situation similar to the one at the "Declaration of Dependence" that I describe in this session? If so, what emotions were you feeling as you stood with your "us" group and faced the "them" group?

3. **Read:** Matthew 9:9–13. What does the fact that Jesus ate with sinners reveal about the way He approached people with the good news? How did He explain His actions to those who didn't understand His methods?

4. **Read:** Luke 7:36–50. Why was Simon, the Pharisee, so offended by Jesus' actions? What did Jesus' response reveal about how He viewed "us" versus "them"?

5. How did Jesus reach out to these individuals in love without endorsing their lifestyles? What concerns would you have about reaching out to unbelievers in the same way?

6. How is God speaking to you about the way in which you view those who are different from you? In what ways do you venture outside your Christian comfort zone to bridge the gap between "us" and "them"?

Closing Prayer

Close your time together in prayer. Here are a few ideas on what you and your group members can pray based on the topic of this session:

○ Pray that God will help you find common ground with those who have beliefs and lifestyles different from your own.

○ Pray that you will be able to follow Jesus' example and model the way He showed love to others.

○ Pray that God will break down any walls that are preventing you from sharing the message of Christ.

○ Pray that you will forgive those who have looked on you as an outsider and that you will continue to see yourself as a new creation in Christ.

Recommended Reading

Review chapter 3, "Us and Them," in *Move On: When Mercy Meets Your Mess.* If you have questions you want to bring to the next meeting, use the space provided below.

*Our job is to love others without stopping to inquire
whether or not they are worthy. That is not our business and,
in fact, it is nobody's business. What we are asked to do is to love,
and this love itself will render both ourselves
and our neighbors worthy.*

Thomas Merton

Between-Sessions Personal Study

DAY 1: **Members Only**

The instructions on the invitations were clear: *Meet at Vicki's backyard tree house at 2:00 p.m. and show your invitation if you want to be in the club.* It was summer break and my best friend and I who were in grade school decided to start a club, likely as an outlet to exert our bossiness. Most every girl in the neighborhood was invited, minus a few that we deemed to be "too young," "too old," or "too annoying." Unfortunately, our first club meeting was also to be our last, thanks to a neighbor mom whose daughter was not invited. She picked up the phone and ratted us out to our mothers, who promptly marched out back and pulled the plug on our exclusive organization.

If we're not careful, those childish urges to exclude can creep into our adult years. And if we're not really careful, we can create our own clubhouse culture in the church. Without even thinking about it, we can create two camps: us and them. Believers and unbelievers. Righteous and sinners. Good and evil. Holy and unholy.

This members-only mentality has been around a long time.

Read: Luke 18:9–14. In the space provided, contrast the actions and attitudes of the two men in this parable.

Tax Collector	Pharisee

Based on what each man said, what was the basis of his relationship with God?

Tax collector:

Pharisee:

What was Jesus' point of the parable?

In the New Testament, Jews often stood to pray, looking toward heaven with their hands lifted, palms up. We can't fault the Pharisee for his physical posture. The rest of his actions? Another story altogether.

Before we condemn the Pharisee for his arrogance, perhaps we'd better do a heart check ourselves.

Have you ever subconsciously been grateful that you weren't like "those" people? You know, them. The "them" that . . .

> Live on the streets.
>
> Are in same-sex relationships.
>
> Have committed crimes.
>
> Have addictions.
>
> Vote differently than you.
>
> Have tattoos and piercings.
>
> Spend their Sundays relaxing or doing yard work rather than going to church.

You get the idea.

Here's another probing question: Have you ever subconsciously (or even consciously) created a list in your head of all the great things you do for God? Things such as . . .

> Teaching a women's Bible study.

Serving at a soup kitchen.

Dropping off a bag of clothes to Goodwill.

Successfully completing a Beth Moore Bible study.

Giving to the building campaign—twice.

Praying out loud in class.

Sponsoring a needy child at Christmas.

God must be happy with your service, right?

And yet, the hero of Jesus' parable wasn't the religious Pharisee. It was a tax collector. Traitor to his people for working for Rome. Hated by his own Jewish brothers for lining his pockets with their hard-earned money. The least likely to be selected for the Righteous Hall of Fame. But Jesus tells us that this guy, not the religious one, went home right before God.

What makes him the hero was his understanding of his own sinfulness. He didn't hide it or cover it up. He didn't deny he had violated the Law. He didn't play games, put on a plastic smile, or nod and say, "I'm fine, how are you?" He knew he was in need of mercy and grace and he wasn't afraid to ask for it. It didn't matter that everyone could see him, but unlike the Pharisee, he wasn't concerned about the applause or the approval of others. The state of his heart was an issue between God and him. Nobody else mattered because nobody else could help. Not even his own "good" works.

That's at the heart of humility, isn't it? Knowing that no matter what we do, our so-called righteousness is nothing but a pile of "filthy rags" (Isaiah 64:6), and that we are all starving beggars needing to be fed by the same Bread of Life.

And that doesn't leave much room for pride.

DAY 2: **Not Invited**

I was in sixth grade when my mother got a call from one of my friend's mothers. I'm not sure she intended me to know the details, but I overheard her telling my father that my friend's mother was concerned that her daughter and I were spending too much time together and it was hindering her daughter from spending time with her "church friends." Bottom line: I wasn't a "church kid." With that one phone call, I learned there was a clear distinction among God's people when it comes to "us" and "them." And you can guess which group I landed in that day. No wonder I wanted nothing to do with Christianity by the time I graduated high school.

Perhaps you can relate to my story. We've all felt the sting of being excluded. And we've all been guilty of excluding others. Jesus had strong words for our tendency as believers to be cliquish and exclusionary.

Read: Luke 19:1–10. A wee little man. A sycamore tree. A shout-out from Jesus. A dinner invitation. Most everyone is familiar with the story of Zacchaeus. What words did Luke use to describe Zacchaeus?

What do you learn about Zacchaeus's character in this story?

How did the people view Zacchaeus?

How did Jesus treat Zacchaeus?

Put yourself in the story. Whom are you most like? Luke, Zacchaeus, the crowd, or Jesus? Explain.

Can you relate to Zacchaeus? If so, describe a time when you felt excluded by "Christians" or cast into the category of "them."

The story of Zacchaeus is in every children's Bible. He's often featured in Backyard Bible Club, VBS, Sunday School, Awana, and children's church. You can't grow up in and around the church without hearing his story zillions of times.

Why? What makes him so special?

One reason, I think, is because Zacchaeus took extreme measures to get a glance of the Messiah. You just don't see many men climbing sycamore trees on the side of the road. He was desperate to find Jesus, so we teach children the importance of going to Jesus.

But that's really not the heart of the story. A subplot, maybe. But not the main takeaway. The real story, the real scandal, is in the interaction between Jesus and Zacchaeus.

Jesus *spoke* to him. Who talks to a tax collector? Everyone—and I mean everyone—hated tax collectors. Slimeballs, all of them. Even more scandalous was that Jesus asked Zacchaeus to stay at his house. Notice that Jesus did the asking, not Zacchaeus. Stay at a tax collector's house? God forbid! That's what the crowd thought, at least. Nobody in that crowd would even treat Zacchaeus with an ounce of respect, much less hang out at his house for pizza and a beer. The crowd saw Zacchaeus as a sinful man to be avoided, not a man in need of reaching (v. 10).

Yes, we learn that Jesus has come to seek and save the lost, but we also get schooled in another important, stereotype-blowing truth: Jesus doesn't leave anybody out. Ever. And neither should we.

Honestly ask yourself: Whom do you leave out? Who is a tax collector, that "sinner" (v. 7) you would rather just avoid and not think about? Here are a few suggestions:

> Your crazy Uncle Harry who insists on debating his political views at family gatherings.

The same-sex parents whose daughter is in your daughter's class at school.

Your eccentric neighbor who insists on displaying a Buddha statue on his front lawn.

Your family member who has been in rehab more times than you can count.

Your friend's son who has a drug addiction.

The single mom who lets her kids run wild in the neighborhood.

The woman at your church who is rumored to have had a string of affairs.

The dad at your kid's sporting event who has a bad habit of cursing.

The girls at your son's high school who dress provocatively.

Our culture is full of sinners. People who aren't in our club because we would never invite them. They'd just muddy up the place. You rub shoulders with them at work, at games, at parties, and even at church. When you see them in the store, you avoid eye contact, pretend you don't see them, and go down another aisle, hoping you don't see them in the parking lot.

We all have our "tax collectors."

Heaven will be full of them.

What a shame if we aren't among those who helped them find their way home.

DAY 3: We the People

I have a family secret. My oldest son and daughter both attended Auburn University. My daughter, however, married in her senior year and her husband took a job in her hometown of Austin. This meant my daughter would have to finish her last year by taking online courses. Unfortunately, Auburn didn't offer the online classes she needed to graduate, but Auburn's rival college did. If you live in the South where football reigns supreme, you understand why my daughter struggled with the decision. The poor child won't even hang up her degree since it is stamped with the seal of her school's archrival.

Us and them. We've been drawing our lines in the sands of time for hundreds and thousands of years. North and South. Pro-life and pro-choice. Activists and pacifists. Black and white. Old and young. Catholic and Protestant. Democrat and Republican. Coke or Pepsi. (Except in the South, where every carbonated beverage is called "a Coke.")

Even in church, we have built walls rather than bridges.

How have you seen the "us versus them" mentality in your experiences in church?

Contemporary or traditional worship style. Sunday school or home groups. Preferred translation of the Bible. Evangelical or charismatic. Pews or theater-style seating. Raised hands in worship or firmly planted by your side. Hymnal or big screen. Men only in church leadership positions or women included. Suits and dresses or blue jeans and T-shirts. Somehow, believers have forgotten the single characteristic that defines and unites us all:

Sinner.

Read: Romans 3:9–12. Several times in this passage, Paul points out that "no one …." List below what he said about "no one."

In verse 9, Paul refers to two groups of people. Who are they? What, in your opinion, would be the modern-day versions of these two groups?

I'm sure Paul ruffled a few Jewish feathers in this letter to the church at Rome. The Jews considered themselves the chosen of God, His children, the righteous remnant from the Old Testament moving forward. And yet, Paul lumped them in with their nonreligious counterparts, the Gentiles. Scandalous.

In Jewish life, the term "Gentile" simply referred to anyone who wasn't a Jew. The term was fairly benign until the New Testament, when the Jews' attitude toward the Gentiles changed. Jews regarded Gentiles with scorn and hatred, calling them unclean enemies of God and His people. Any child born of a Jew-Gentile marriage was considered a bastard.[12] Yikes. Talk about us versus them.

Yet against this cultural background, Paul set forth a new theology: There is no difference between Jew and Gentile (or Greek)—all are under sin (v. 9). All of us are in the same predicament, and all of us face the same judgment. And God provided a solution for all of us.

> For all have sinned and fall short of the glory of God. They are justified freely by His grace through the redemption that is in Christ Jesus.
>
> (Romans 3:23–24 HCSB)

Did you find the solution? Underline it.

We're all sinners. All of us. The Sunday school teacher and the neo-Nazi. Your pastor and the pedophile. The medical missionary and the crackhead. The Bible study leader and the abortionist. God's Word is clear about this. Nobody gets a free pass. There are no levels of sin in God's eyes. Sin is sin. You are no better than the neighbor who abuses his wife. Yes, the consequences for sin in this life are different. But the wages of sin are still the same—death. And the offer of forgiveness is given to all, including that abortionist and pedophile.

Do you find yourself lumping people into two categories of "us" and "them"? Maybe just a little bit?

When you and I allow pride to take root in our hearts, the fruit is self-righteous arrogance. We divide the world into US and THEM. We are on God's side and those who disagree with us—even if they claim to be Christians—belong on the other team.

The truth of the matter is that we're all equal at the foot of the cross. There is no us and them. There are no brownie points for visiting shut-ins, no coupons for teaching third grade Sunday school, no "get out of jail free" cards because we have never been arrested. The Bible is clear: no one is righteous based on his or her own actions. Nobody.

We've all sinned. We all need God's forgiveness through Christ alone. All of "us." And "them."

"We" are all equals at the foot of the cross.

DAY 4: The Least of These

Back when I was in high school in the early '80s, the homecoming court was predictably comprised of the popular girls who were cheerleaders or drill team captains. That is, until my graduating class came along and broke the trend. My class decided to change up the rules a bit and throw everyone for a loop. Oh sure, there was still a slate of popular, pretty girls who made the cut, but one girl didn't fit the mold. She was a punk rocker with short, blonde, spiked hair whose wardrobe was comprised of one color: black. It caused quite a stir when she got nominated and even more of a stir when she was crowned homecoming queen. Even though I voted for my best friend and fellow cheerleader, a part of me loved the fact that my class had dared to be different and do the unexpected.

One of the most polarizing aspects of Jesus' ministry was that He refused to play by the rules when it came to the religious customs of the day.

He healed a woman on the Sabbath, which was considered "work" and therefore prohibited (Luke 13:10–17).

He and His disciples ate grain on the Sabbath, which was also a no-no (Matthew 12:1–8).

He held a religious conversation with a Samaritan woman (John 4).

He called out the Pharisees and religious leaders for their hypocrisy (Matthew 23).

He touched a leper (Mark 1:40–45) and set free a demon-possessed man (Mark 5:1–17).

He constantly crashed through every religious, social, and cultural boundary constructed by the leaders of His day.

Read: Mark 2:13–17. It'll sound somewhat familiar to you. List all the groups of people Jesus associated with.

Paraphrase the response of the religious elite.

You have already learned about Zacchaeus, another famous tax collector in the Gospels. Two different men, but the same response from both—immediately they followed Jesus. Two different men, but the same response from the scribes and Pharisees: How dare he!

The religious leaders of the day had strayed so far from the teachings of the Old Testament that they were actually indignant at His correct interpretation of the Scriptures. The Jewish people were supposed to be lights to other nations. They were chosen, yes, but chosen for a task that was abandoned for empty rituals and meaningless sacrifices.

Even His disciples found themselves rebuked by their Master for trying to fold Him into culture's mold.

> Some people were bringing little children to Him so He might touch them, but His disciples rebuked them. When Jesus saw it, He was indignant and said to them, "Let the little children come to Me. Don't stop them, for the kingdom of God belongs to such as these. I assure you: Whoever does not welcome the kingdom of God like a little child will never enter it." After taking them in His arms, He laid His hands on them and blessed them.
>
> (MARK 10:13–16 HCSB)

Jesus constantly reached out to the marginalized and the outcast. From the woman caught in adultery to a bunch of unschooled, roughneck fishermen, He redeemed the unredeemable and recognized the forgotten. He even used the most heinously hated—Saul turned Paul—to become His mouthpiece of the gospel and chief writer of the New Testament.

A murderer. A tax collector. A harlot. A half-breed Samaritan.

Only the Savior could redeem those who had been rejected by culture for not being good enough. Only the Creator could see in broken people His original design and purpose in them. Only the Bridegroom could see His beloved's beauty beneath the soot of sin.

As His disciples, He calls us to do the same.

Care for those forgotten and condemned by culture. The single mom on welfare. The newly paroled man. The pregnant teenager. The socially awkward woman who sits behind you in church. We are called to tear down those walls and love as He loved.

Love the sinner and hate the sin for how it destroys the sinner.

Not hate the sinner and ignore our own sin.

Unfortunately, we've become experts at that.

DAY 5: **Final Words**

He hugged me and with a confident reassurance said, "Remember, this isn't 'goodbye' … only 'see ya later.'" Those were the last and final words my literary agent spoke to me just weeks before he was ushered into glory after a two-year battle with brain cancer. I will never forget them.

Last words. Sometimes funny, sometimes poignant. Always memorable. The parting words of loved ones sink deeply into our hearts and sear themselves deep into our brains for further recall and remembrance.

What famous last words of a friend or loved one do you still remember? Or perhaps someone in history?

Why do you think last words stay with us so long?

When sitting beside a friend who has only a few days to live, time stops. Every nanosecond matters. The world may be racing by at warp speed, but your world has slowed to a stop, allowing you to intentionally live in that moment. You soak in every memory, every shared smile, every word spoken.

John 15:9–17 contains one of the last conversations between Jesus and His disciples (John 19 records His crucifixion). Jesus had His heart and His path set toward Jerusalem. He knew the cross would soon separate Him from the disciples. While they didn't understand that they were characters in the greatest story ever told, Jesus knew. And because He knew what lay ahead, every statement that flowed across His lips held deep, deep significance.

Read: John 15:9–17. Now go back and count every time the word "love" is used in this passage. How many did you find?

In these verses (vv. 12, 17), Jesus repeated a command. What was it?

Why do you think Jesus gave this particular command?

To what degree are we to love others? (just as ...)

"Love each other as I have loved you." Jesus could have listed out any litany of commands for the disciples to follow—the laws from the Old Testament, a review of one of His sermons, a warning about what they would endure as first-century martyrs. But He didn't.

"Love each other as I have loved you." Jesus didn't tell the disciples to picket at the entrance of the temples in Rome. He didn't command them to start a boycott. He never mentioned forming a political party to fight against moral corruption.

"Love each other as I have loved you." That command still applies to us today. He didn't call us to act as judge and jury for Him. He told us that others would know our love for Christ by our love for others (John 13:35). A patient love. A gentle love. A "love them in their mess" kind of love. Yes, Jesus spoke against sin. Yes, He told people to leave their sinful lives behind. However, He treated sinners with deep love, a love He did not demonstrate to the religious elite. That ought to tell us something.

What might happen if we spent our money and our time on a home for unwed mothers instead of picketing abortion clinics?

What if we stopped complaining about the moral decay of our country and funneled our energy into finding a way to be part of the solution?

What if we quit ranting about the unemployed "freeloaders" who are taking advantage of our tax dollars and found a way to mentor them instead?

What if we demonstrated to our children how to love others instead of fearing them? Condemning them? Judging them?

For God so loved the world ...

Move On Challenge

Spend some time in prayer as you take an honest inventory of groups you have been guilty of labeling as "them." Ask God to help you "cross the line" and take a first step toward loving them and engaging with them, rather than judging them from the sidelines. What specific ideas come to mind?

Law and Disorder

Legalism is joyless because it's endless.
There's always another class to attend.
Inmates incarcerated in self-salvation
find work, but never joy!
Grace offers rest. Legalism? Never!

MAX LUCADO

Welcome

Welcome to session four of *Move On: When Mercy Meets Your Mess.* Before watching the video, briefly discuss with each other what has been happening in your lives during the week. Also discuss any key points that stood out to you from the between-sessions personal study and any questions that came up since the last session.

Video Teaching

As you watch the video for session four, use the following outline to record any thoughts or concepts that stand out to you.

Many of the absurd laws we find in America can likely be traced back to one person with a hyper-legalistic sense of justice imposing his or her personal preference on the general public. In a way, this is similar to the type of legalism that some Christians try to impose on others today.

When our faith reaches a point where it becomes more focused on rules than on grace, we become trapped in an endless cycle of dos and don'ts and shoulds and shouldn'ts. As believers set free in Christ, why do we have a tendency to hitch these long lists of rules to God's amazing grace?

God's grace amounts to "Jesus + nothing," while legalism is "Jesus + some things." The sad truth is that many of us didn't allow this concept of grace to seep into our souls and become the foundation of our faith. In fact, the primary root of legalism boils down to an improper understanding of God's grace.

The goal of legalists is to toe the line spiritually according to a self-imposed list of rules and regulations. Even though they've been set free from the law, they choose to remain in the prison yard of their own rigid guidelines. Unfortunately, they are not content to remain in that prison yard alone while other Christians dare to live in freedom.

What is our default, gut-level, go-to reaction when we see or hear of a fellow believer engaging in a "liberty" with which we don't personally agree?

When we imagine that God shakes His head with disdain every time we fail to perform, we will respond by either performing out of fear or distancing ourselves from God. Either way, we will remain in the prison yard.

The Great Commission calls us to make disciples of Jesus, not recruit others to a works-based lifestyle that makes *us* feel better and makes *them* feel like constant failures.

Without grace, Christianity ceases to be different from any other works-based religion. Christianity without grace is powerless.

Small Group Discussion

Take some time at this point to discuss with your fellow group members what you just watched and to explore these concepts in Scripture.

1. What was your initial response when you heard about some of the strange-but-true laws in the United States? How do you think the individuals responsible for thinking up these laws were able to convince lawmakers to enact them?

2. Where would you rank yourself in regard to being legalistic? What standards have you set for yourself that have led to grace equaling "Jesus + some things"?

3. **Read:** Galatians 3:23–25. What does Paul say was the purpose of the "law"—the Old Testament rules and regulations? What has happened now that Christ has come?

4. **Read:** Romans 6:1–2 and Titus 2:11–12. As Christians, do we have the right to just disregard the law? To what place should grace lead us in our walk with God?

5. In what ways have you been guilty of imposing your self-made rules for Christianity on others? How have other Christians attempted to impose their rules on you?

6. In what ways have you imposed similar legalistic rules on yourself? How do you discover God's grace when you find yourself feeling as if you do not measure up?

Closing Prayer

Close your time together in prayer. Here are a few ideas on what you and your group members can pray based on the topic of this session:

- Pray that you will allow God's grace to seep into your soul and become the foundation of your faith.

- Pray that God will set you free from imposing self-made rules on yourself and others.

- Pray that God will lead you to a place of grateful obedience to the work and discipline He is doing in your life.

- Pray that God will help you to always first extend grace to others.

Recommended Reading

Review chapter 6, "Law and Disorder," in *Move On: When Mercy Meets Your Mess.* If you have questions you want to bring to the next meeting, use the space provided below.

You do not become a master musician
by playing just as you please,
by imagining that learning the scales
is sheer legalism and bondage!
No, true freedom in any area of life
is the consequence of regular discipline.

SINCLAIR B. FERGUSON

Between-Sessions Personal Study

DAY 1: The Root of Legalism

I'm a recovering legalist. There, I said it. After years of living by a list of self-imposed rules (and expecting you to live by the same narrow list), I finally buckled under the weight of the burden. I just couldn't do it any longer. Somewhere along the way, I became more concerned with living by a list of rules than living in light of redemption. I was stuck in an endless cycle of ritualistic performance where I somehow imagined a God who was grading me each and every day. If I felt it was an A- to an A+ day, I felt good. Unfortunately, those days were rare. There were point deductions for not reading my Bible or praying. There were point deductions for failing to turn the conversation to Christ with my neighbor or missing church on Sunday. Deduct more points for watching a secular TV show, failing to tithe 10 percent, and not signing up for evangelism training at the church. When you begin to base God's love on a pass/fail system, it's only a matter of time before the joy of your salvation is replaced with an obligation to maintain your salvation.

Nobody aspires to be a soul-killing legalist. You don't wake up one morning and think to yourself, "Gee, I think I'll replace dynamic relationship with stoic rules and rituals. I'll be so much happier if I adhere to a list of dos and don'ts that even the most saintly saint can't live up to." For most people, legalism is a gradual slide, like the proverbial frog in the kettle.

Legalism refers to the emphasis on laws or codes of conduct in order to earn God's favor, His forgiveness, or His attention. It is the mistaken idea that in order to be a "good" Christian, I must follow the "rules" in the Bible, as well as the rules I create (or your church establishes).

Seeking to follow God's Word because you love God doesn't make you a legalist. Following the Bible so you feel better and look good is legalistic. See the difference? One focuses on your relationship with God, while the other focuses on your own merit and actions.

Legalism was a problem in both the Old and New Testaments, although the word "legalism" itself doesn't occur in any of the books. In fact, the book of Isaiah opens with God's disgust at following the Law at the expense of loving Him and loving others.

Read: Isaiah 1:11–18 and take note of the elements of legalism you discover. In the space below, record what you find.

Unfortunately, the vast majority of Jewish people and their leaders continued in their empty religious practices while simultaneously rebelling against God. In fact, not much had changed when Jesus began His ministry. Some of His harshest indictments were leveled at self-righteous Jews who thought that their sacrifices and offerings justified them before God and made them better than the common "sinner."

Check out what Jesus said to the Pharisees and the teachers of the law in Matthew:

> You hypocrites! Isaiah was right when he prophesied about you: "These people honor me with their lips, but their hearts are far from me. They worship me in vain; their teachings are merely human rules."
>
> (MATTHEW 15:7–9)

Ouch.

Was Jesus telling the people not to follow the Ten Commandments? Not at all.

Was He trying to put the Law in proper perspective? Absolutely.

Look up Matthew 15:9b in the following translations and jot down other phrases used for "human rules":

English Standard Version _____

The Message _____

New Living Translation _____

Off the top of your head, list below some common "man-made rules" that are mistakenly taught as doctrine when it comes to the Christian faith.

In Galatians 3, Paul explained that God gave the law (think Old Testament rules and regulations, sacrifices, rites, etc.) so that all of us would know how sinful we really are. It's our measuring stick, showing us how far away from God we have all strayed. That understanding of our depravity should lead us to faith in Christ, not to more useless deeds that can't wipe away the stain of sin. The law itself does not offer freedom, but it does point to the Giver of freedom (John 8:32).

The problem comes when you and I get the two confused, when we take our focus off of the cross and place it on our own "good" deeds. And once we slide into the dank prison of legalism, we'll be shackled there as long as we believe that our actions earn us a spot in heaven.

Legalism says, "I don't need your sacrifice, Jesus. I can do this on my own."

Faith says, "Have mercy on me, Son of God. I can't do this on my own."

Which declaration have you made? You may be surprised.

DAY 2: **Harmful If Swallowed**

They were called "Radium Girls," young women hired by watch-making factories to paint radium-lit watch faces primarily for the military between 1917–1926. Told the material was not harmful, many of the women would put it in their mouths to re-form the brush tip after several applications. For fun, many of the Radium Girls painted their teeth, nails, and faces, fascinated by the magical glowing product. It wasn't until years later when many of them became ill, suffering from anemia, bone fractures, and necrosis of the jaw that the radioactive paint was found to be poisonous. Because it had been ingested in such small doses, the women never suspected the harm it was doing to their systems over time.

In a similar way, legalism can seep into our lives unnoticed and poison our belief system. As a new believer in Jesus, you want to know God more, so you spend time in worship and prayer and reading the Bible. You want to go to church and know more about this gospel that has set your heart free. Over time, though, if you're not careful, something else creeps in. Slowly, very slowly, microscopic seeds of pride begin to scatter across your heart. The thoughts begin benignly, with phrases like, "Wow! I'm learning so much!" and "I can't believe I used to live that way!" You are learning and you are changing. However, if the focus ever shifts from what God has done to what you have done, then the seeds are beginning to take root. If left unchecked, those seeds will suck out any love you used to hold for God and will leave you hard-hearted. Cold. Cynical. Judgmental.

Read: Matthew 23:1–4, 23–28 to learn from the Who's Who of Legalism. In the chart below, in the left column list the things Jesus noted as legalistic and hypocritical. Then in the right column, write down how some of those things (like burdening people) might be manifested by legalists today. I've given you an example.

Jesus' Indictment	Modern-day Examples
"They don't practice what they teach"	Someone who tells you not to gossip but gossips, too

Jesus provided vivid descriptions of the Pharisees, leaving no doubt about their behavior. In verse 4, Jesus spoke of heavy loads that are hard to carry. It was a picture the New Testament Jew would understand—burdening an animal with a heavy load, almost to the brink. That's legalism—a constant burden that we place on others.

Unfortunately, some of us have laid some heavy burdens on others with our outrageous expectations. I've been guilty. I'm sure you have, too. Expecting new believers not to swear on occasion. Judging "church kids" when they make a moral failure. Refusing to help someone in need because that need was a consequence of sin, like snubbing a woman who gets pregnant out of wedlock. That judgmental spirit is sure to draw her to Jesus.

The Pharisees were worried about tithing their spices but couldn't be bothered with more central matters—like justice and mercy.

Guilty. Have you attended church on Sunday morning more out of a sense of obligation? Are you there to mark it off your list or hear from God? Are you more concerned with maintaining your image or maintaining your heart?

Stop for a minute and consider the spiritual disciplines in your life. Which ones, if any, might you be performing out of a sense of duty? If you are struggling with answering this question, ask yourself which duties, if not performed, would leave you with a sense of guilt.

Whether we want to admit it or not, it's easy to play the Pharisee. Expecting others to meet our expectations. Worrying about what others think. Judging others for their sin, while forgetting our own.

God never intended for us to be in the prison of legalism. Nor did He intend for us to appoint ourselves as the prison guards. And the scary part is this: we can be both the captive and the captor at the same time.

DAY 3: Get Out of Jail Free (Sort of)

You've probably played the board game "Monopoly," especially if you have kids. It's the game that can go on forever. The goal, of course, is to create a monopoly of the properties and utilities on the board, while also acquiring a mass of wealth and houses and hotels.

Two of the most coveted cards you can draw in the game are the "Get Out of Jail Free" cards—one in the Chance stack and one in the Community Chest stack. Throughout the game, a player may land himself in jail. Obviously, this card releases you from your pretend confinement and you can continue on in the game. Without it, you must wait three turns (unless you roll doubles on any of those turns), and after the third roll, you must pay a fine of $50 to get out of jail. While in jail, you cannot collect rent or buy or sell properties, so it's a stinky place to be.

If you had the "Get Out of Jail Free" card, you wouldn't stick around in jail just for fun. Nor would you pay the fifty bucks if you didn't have to. That would be stupid.

So is trying to earn God's favor with your acts of service and sacrifice.

Read: Galatians 3:1–9. What did Paul call the Galatian Christians (vv. 1, 3)?

What was the reason for his harsh rebuke?

How do believers receive the Spirit? How are they considered righteous before God?

What does it mean to "be made complete by the flesh"? (v. 3 HCSB) What are some examples?

Nobody likes to be called out as foolish, and yet that's exactly how Paul described the believers at Galatia. Why? Because they had initially received Christ by faith but then subsequently slipped into a works-oriented life-style. A group of people called Judaizers (Jewish Christians) had infiltrated the small church and had been telling new Gentile Christians that they must follow Jewish law (circumcision, food laws, Sabbath observance, etc.) in order to be saved.

Does it sound eerily familiar? Obviously, you're not going to hear a sermon in your local church on the necessity of circumcision in order to follow Jesus. However, that same mentality can be spotted in just about every denomination.

It sounds like this:

"I don't smoke, cuss, or chew, or hang around people who do."

"You can't really call yourself a Christian if you listen to that stuff."

"Christian parents should not let their kids read or watch *Harry Potter, Twilight, Hunger Games,* etc."

"That other denomination can't be right. What we believe is the real truth."

"Real Christians can't get depressed when they have the joy of the Lord."

"The King James Version is the only accurate version of Scripture."

"As long as I don't _____ (insert big sins here: lie, murder, or commit adultery), then I'm okay."

"You should read your Bible every morning before you start your day."

Can you think of an example of a legalism that you have embraced? If so, what is it?

At the time, did you recognize it as legalism or did you buy in on some level?

Each of the examples in the list above focuses on outward action. Doing. Or NOT doing. Just read your Bible daily and fill your iPod with praise music. And never watch an R-rated movie. Or enjoy a glass of wine. Or thumb through a gossip magazine. Or slip and say "hell" instead of "heck." Toe the line. Follow the rules. Living this way is like continually trying to roll for doubles to get out of jail when you've already been given the card to get out.

I'm not trying to make light of the enormity of Christ's sacrifice by comparing it to a board game. I am trying to highlight the futility of living shackled by the chains of performance-based "Christianity," which is really a perversion of the gospel.

The whole reason the Eternal Word became human and pitched His tent among us was because we could never perform well enough to earn the right to be called God's own. God won't save us because we went to enough conferences, volunteered in the nursery, and sent our children to a Christian private school. He saves us because we cannot save ourselves.

His grace is free, but it came with an exorbitant price.

How great the Father's love for us … and yet we spurn His love so we can return to our prison cells that feel more familiar and comfortable than a life of grace.

Jesus has handed you a "Get Out of Jail Free" card. Why do you remain in your cell?

DAY 4: **Finding the Key**

One of the most powerful scenes in the epic movie, *Chronicles of Narnia: The Lion, the Witch, and the Wardrobe,* takes place at the end of the story when Aslan rescues the creatures who have been frozen by the White Witch. With breaths from his mouth, the Lion melts each and every creature and brings it back to life.

Not only is this a beautiful portrayal of the gospel, but it is also a stunning image of how Christ can set us free from legalism. With one breath from His mouth, He warms us against cold religiosity. We come alive in His presence when His Spirit blows life into our hardened hearts. We are no longer frozen by our past mistakes and others' unrealistic expectations but are released instead to walk in the glorious freedom of the children of God.

Unfortunately, many of our fellow Christ followers have been frozen by the icy hands of legalism, and often we have been part of the problem. We have placed expectations on them. We have failed to leave the past in the past. We focus on their outward behavior instead of being concerned about their inward condition. Fortunately, that doesn't have to be the end of the story. As God begins to change our hearts and warm them toward Him, we can offer the same warmth and grace to others. We can help them come alive and find the same freedom that has liberated us.

Read: Romans 14:1–12. What do you think Paul meant by those "whose faith is weak"?

Why do you think Paul told us not to "quarrel about disputable matters" ("argue about doubtful issues," HCSB)?

What was Paul's solution for those "doubtful issues"?

How would you summarize verse 4 in today's language?

How does verse 4 relate to verses 10–12?

In the South, they say, "You ain't got a dog in this hunt." Translation? Mind your own business.

That's the essence of what Paul wrote in Romans 14.

One of the best ways we can offer life to others is to simply stop trying to dictate how they should live. Instead, we need to focus on our own relationship with the Lord, and give others the same freedom as well. While visiting with one of my fellow author friends recently, she said something about legalism that was profound. She said, "The old brand of legalism (peddled mainly by the older generation) focuses on what you shouldn't do. The new brand of legalism (peddled mainly by the younger generation) focuses on what you should be doing."

In a nutshell, we've moved from "Good Christians shouldn't _____" to "Good Christians should _____." This truth was proven at a recent conference where I was the speaker. After the event a young mother approached me and, through tears, shared that she was buckling under a pressure she felt at her church to … take in foster children, adopt children, wear jewelry and scarves made only by women in third world countries, give the bulk of her income to the poor, and take up the latest social injustice cause. I am certainly not suggesting Christians shouldn't do these things (if so led), but we need to respect that not everyone is called to engage in the same cause(s). And we need to seriously examine our hearts to see if we have played a part in guilting others who don't share our same convictions.

Ask yourself:

○ *Who am I to tell someone else what God's Spirit is telling them?*

○ *Why do I think others should act the same way I do? Dress like I do?*

○ *Why do I think others should agree with my political position in order to be a "real Christian"?*

○ *How often do I focus on the faults and flaws of others instead of paying attention to my own, asking God for the grace to be more like Him?*

○ *What would my family be like if I spent more time encouraging them instead of complaining every time someone doesn't fulfill my demands?*

○ *How often do I demonstrate love toward "sinners" instead of passing judgment?*

○ *Why do I think others need to live up to my expectations?*

Can you imagine standing before Christ at the foot of the cross and speaking aloud the words of judgment and condemnation that we often harbor in our hearts? Can you imagine being in the presence of God and complaining that others don't act like we do? Such scenarios are unfathomable.

One key to offering our brothers and sisters freedom is to drop the chains we bind up around them and to let them pursue their own relationship with God without our running commentary. God doesn't need our help in transforming lives. He can do just fine without us.

Each person is held accountable to the Lord. They are certainly not accountable to me—or to you.

Let's get out of the way and let God do His work as He sees fit, not according to our own myopic perspectives.

DAY 5: **Free at Last**

"If I could go back and do it over again ... " We've all said it, especially if you're a parent. Do-overs. Mulligans. Reboots. Second chances. Everyone needs the opportunity to start over again because we all mess up. We miss the mark, fall short, fail, falter, and stumble. If not given a second (and third and fourth ...) chance, none of us would ever get out of bed in the morning. We certainly wouldn't try to approach God.

Perhaps that's why God inspired the writers to pen the words from today's study. We all need reassurance that failure is not the last word.

Read: Micah 7:18–19. In the space below, draw a picture that summarizes these two verses.

What a beautiful picture. The God of the Universe takes our sins, tramples them underfoot (remember Genesis 3:15), and then hurls them all into the depths of the sea. The deepest part of the ocean is called the Mariana Trench. It's almost seven miles deep. To give you perspective, if Mount Everest were placed on the bottom of the trench, there would still be a mile of water above its peak.[13] It's as if God is saying, "I'm going to separate you from your sin as far as possible." Why use this illustration? To show us that no matter how deep the sin, His grace and love are deeper still. We can wake up again the next morning without the weight of our sin on our shoulders because that sin is long gone.

Every new day, every new moment gives us another chance.

Read: Lamentations 3:22–24. Put these verses in your own words as a prayer of thanks to God.

My body bears the marks of getting older. Bifocals. New wrinkles. New crackles and pops when I get out of bed in the morning. More aches and pains than in my twenties, for sure. The earth shows marks of getting older. So does every house, building, car, and computer. Over time, things just naturally decay. Wear. Tear. Fade. Weaken.

Everything, that is, except God's mercy.

This beautiful poem, penned by the prophet Jeremiah, is a reminder that while everything else may change, God's mercy is constant. In fact, it is new every morning. Fresh. Full and brimming over. Available in abundance.

Friend, you may feel as if God is weary of your weakness. You may be frustrated because you stumbled yet AGAIN. You may wonder if God's love has limits. Rest assured, He has more than enough love for you. You cannot out-sin God's mercy. You cannot make Him love you any more than He does in this very moment—and you cannot make Him love you any less. His love for you is perfect.

To stay out of the prison of legalism, you and I must believe and act upon promises like these in Scripture. We must lay our sins at the foot of the cross and leave them there. Refuse to take them back up again. Allow Him to hurl them into the Mariana Trench.

It's a new day with new mercy.

How will you spend it? In regret and remorse over sin that has already been forgiven and forgotten (Isaiah 43:24)? Or in wonder and worship of a God whose grace is abundant and whose love is never-ending?

The choice is yours.

Move On Challenge

Identify three areas where you have a tendency to be legalistic. What types of things have you said/thought in the past when confronted with these three areas? What would it look like to change the "old tapes"? Write down below what you might say/think the next time you are confronted with the temptation to be legalistic in one of these areas.

Buzz-Hopping

*God put a longing for unfailing love in our hearts
because He knew it would lead us back to Him.
Only God's unfailing love will fill and fulfill the desires of our hearts.
It is the deepest thirst of our souls.
Until God's love is enough, nothing else will be.*

RENEE SWOPE

Welcome

Welcome to session five of *Move On: When Mercy Meets Your Mess*. Before watching the video, briefly discuss with each other what has been happening in your lives during the week. Also discuss any key points that stood out to you from the between-sessions personal study and any questions that came up since the last session.

Video Teaching

As you watch the video for session five, use the following outline to record any thoughts or concepts that stand out to you.

The false gods we chase offer a temporary buzz of satisfaction, but it is always short-lived. Unless we find our satisfaction in God, we'll just end up empty.

The truth is we are no different than the Israelites in the wilderness. Like junkies in need of a fix, we hop from one buzz to another, looking for something to satisfy our souls.

When we become more enamored with the *created* rather than the *Creator*, we are at risk of creating our own golden calves. Our golden calves can take the shape of things such as food, drugs, the number of digits on a paycheck, or even the digits on the scale.

Idols can almost always be traced back to what began as a mismanaged or mishandled craving. This craving is not by accident. God has wired our hearts to seek satisfaction and fulfillment, but He intended we find it in Him first and foremost.

According to author Tim Keller, an idol is anything more important to us than God, anything that absorbs our heart and imagination more than God, and anything we seek to give us what only God can give.

Life is messy, and a mere declaration of love isn't enough to carry us through the hard times. When we fail to stoke the fire, the flame will eventually die.

God wants us to *remember* and *repent*. He wants us to reflect on that moment when His grace and mercy intersected our lives—and He wants us to go back to that place often.

If we don't resolve to cling to God and fight with every fiber of our being to hang on, we will tether our hearts to shifting shadows and false gods that won't deliver. If we want to keep our love for God alive, we must *fight* to keep it alive.

Small Group Discussion

Take some time at this point to discuss with your fellow group members what you just watched and to explore these concepts in Scripture.

1. In the introduction to this session, I share about a dish at one of my favorite restaurants: the Marsha's Special. When my husband and I push away from the table, we are fully satisfied ... for a few hours. How is the same true when we chase after false gods? Why do idols never really satisfy?

2. **Read:** Exodus 19:3–8 and 32:1–6. God had blessed the Israelites and guided them out of Egypt, and at Mount Sinai they had promised to serve Him. So why did they so quickly turn to worshiping idols at the first sign of trouble? What is our own susceptibility to being drawn to the allure of false gods when the storms of life arrive?

3. Ralph Waldo Emerson is credited with saying, "A person will worship something, have no doubt about that." What types of things tend to preoccupy your time? What do you daydream the most about? Are these things idols to you?

4. **Read:** Revelation 2:2–5. For what did Jesus commend the people in this church in Ephesus? What did He hold against them?

5. In what ways are you "going through the motions" in your worship of God? How are you fighting to keep the flame of your love for Him alive?

6. What are some tangible steps you can take to guard against the idols that threaten to become the object of your primary affection? Who can keep you accountable to take these steps and let you know when an idol is creeping into your life?

Closing Prayer

Close your time together in prayer. Here are a few ideas on what you and your group members can pray based on the topic of this session:

○ Pray that God will help you to not be more enamored with the created rather than the Creator Himself.

○ Pray that God will reveal to you any mismanaged or mishandled cravings you have.

○ Pray that God will lead you to reflect often on the moment when His mercy met your mess and to remember your first love for Him.

○ Pray that God will help you fight to keep the idols out of your life.

Recommended Reading

Review chapter 8, "Buzz-Hopping," in *Move On: When Mercy Meets Your Mess*. If you have questions you want to bring to the next meeting, use the space provided below.

When told to shut out the world from his heart,
this may be impossible with him who has nothing to replace it —
but not impossible with him who has found
in God a sure and satisfying portion.

THOMAS CHALMERS

Between-Sessions Personal Study

DAY 1: Big G versus Little g's

Panic. It was the morning of the annual "field day" at my elementary school. I was determined to retain my title of "fastest girl in the fifth grade," but my good-luck track shoes were nowhere to be found. I'd probably left them at a friend's house, but it was too late to locate them in time for the competition. I had begged and begged for these running shoes months prior and even slept in them the first night after finally getting them. I had never lost a race without them. I had no choice but to wear my old, clunky tennis shoes to field day. I came in second place that day and was convinced it was because I was missing my good-luck shoes. Today, it seems ridiculous that I put so much trust in a silly pair of rubber track shoes. Like the Israelites in the Old Testament, we too are prone to fashioning idols out of ridiculous objects and expecting them to deliver in the way of favorable results.

Talking about idols in the twenty-first century seems a little out of place. Idols are the stuff of a documentary on the History Channel, where people dig in dusty deserts to uncover some fertility god in the ancient sands of Saudi Arabia. Our current world is too advanced, too sophisticated, and too intelligent to ever think that any power could come from an object, right? Maybe not. (We'll get to that later.) On the contrary, discussing idols is as relevant now as in Old Testament times, where at least a dozen different idols are mentioned by its various authors.[14]

From the beginning of His relationship with the nation of Israel, God spoke against the idea of worshiping idols and false gods. He made His feelings very clear.

Read: Exodus 20:3–6. What explicit commands did God set forth in these verses?

When you read the command against making an idol, what picture comes into your head?

What do you think God meant when He said He is a "jealous God"?

God's commands couldn't have been clearer: Don't have other gods besides me. And don't bow down to other gods, giving them your allegiance and affection. End of discussion.

Why would God include these commands in the Ten Commandments? Why would He care about idols or other gods, especially since they aren't real anyway? The answer lies in the character of God. He is a "jealous" God. The word is used only six times in the Old Testament, and all of them refer to God.[15] The word implies that God will not allow a rival to Himself.[16] Again, this begs the question, why? First, God deserves single-hearted devotion. He is Almighty God and to say that something else is worthy of worship is an affront to His holiness. Second, God wants our devotion. He has expressed His consistent love to us, much like a husband to his new bride, and longs for us to respond in love.

Read: Deuteronomy 6:5–9. What is God's plea in these verses?

Why would He want us to impart this command to our children?

Does this command sound familiar? If not, **Read:** Mark 12:28–31. Why do you think Jesus restated this command?

By the time Jesus hit the streets of Jerusalem, Judaism had drifted away from its love and allegiance to God, especially among the scribes and religious leaders who asked Him the question in the first place. Yes, the temple stood imposing and impressive in the city (but not for long). Yes, the people offered the required sacrifices under the Law of Moses. And yes, they offered the required offering. But God wasn't concerned with sacrifices, places of worship, or offerings. He didn't care about bulls or shekels. He was after something far more important, far more valuable.

Read: Matthew 15:7–9. Based on these verses, what does God want?

God wants your heart. Your devotion. Your affection. Anything that steals your affection away from God is an idol. Anything. Statue or not, idolatry is principally a matter of the heart. What holds your attention? What are your emotions, time, money, and thoughts focused on? Devoted to? That's your god. And if it's not Almighty God (Big G), then it's a thousand other little gods (lowercase g). We'll talk about them tomorrow.

For today, ask yourself, *What am I devoted to?*

DAY 2: **When God Tarries**

The waiting game. At some point in our lives, we will find ourselves sitting in God's waiting room anxiously awaiting an answer or His intervention. When will I meet the man of my dreams? When will I finally get pregnant? When will my family member be healed? When will I lose this weight? When … when … when? Whether we realize it or not, many of us have written scripts for our lives and assigned God the part of chief genie. Yet when He doesn't show up or deliver in the way we imagined, we find ourselves sitting in the waiting room growing more confused as the days go by. "Where is He?" "Why is He not answering my prayers in the way I had imagined?"

When God tarries, we become easy prey for a multitude of false gods that promise to deliver.

Yesterday, we read the most familiar passage (perhaps) in the Old Testament—the Ten Commandments. Early on in His covenant relationship with the Israelites, God clearly commanded the people not to have any other gods besides Him. We discovered yesterday that God is a jealous God and wants our single-hearted devotion. However, a story that takes place just after Moses received the Ten Commandments reveals another reason God made such a command. Like us, the Israelites found themselves sitting in God's waiting room awaiting His intervention. And when He tarried and didn't deliver according to their timeline and script, it wasn't pretty.

Read: Exodus 32:1–6, 19–24. What did the people want?

Why did the people want it?

Why do you think Aaron complied with their request?

What takes place after the idol is created?

When does Moses enter the picture?

What is Aaron's explanation?

Forty days. That's how long the people had to wait for Moses as he received the Ten Commandments. Apparently, forty days was just too much. When Moses didn't show up fast enough, the people got impatient. They wanted a new god to follow, one they could see and touch and rally around. One that other nations could see and admire and fear. Though Yahweh God had delivered them from the hand of the Egyptians and rescued them from one problem after another, they still doubted Him. Their faith was weak, their trust anemic.

Remember, the command against other gods was being written on the stone tablets up on the mountain. At the same time, the people are screaming at Aaron to give them a new and improved god. With God and Moses up on the mountain, the people down below are living like God doesn't exist. Moses was a no-show and his God was absent too. So let the pagan party rock on. From the mountain, God saw it all.

He knew the Israelites would be easily enticed to follow after gods of the surrounding peoples, gods such as Baal, Asherah, Artemis, and Ashtoreth. These gods would seem more appealing. More easily controlled. More popular. Perhaps that's why God set forth the command—because He knew just how often we would break it. Again and again.

You and I may laugh at the picture of the Israelites dancing around a golden calf. We might judge their behavior as ignorant and ill-informed. After all, who would believe that an inanimate object could really provide good crops? Why would anyone think a sculpture had the power to heal disease or cure infertility? How stupid, right?

Before you answer that, you might want to step back and look at our own culture. It is steeped in its own gods, but with more familiar names. We're guilty of idolatry, but it's couched in terms like "priorities" and "hobbies" and "career" and "children." Oh, we're dancing around our own calves, but we just describe it as the American Way.

DAY 3: **Idols in the Spotlight**

Yesterday, we examined Israel's abandonment of God in favor of a golden calf. Unfortunately, the Old Testament records that the tendency to ditch God was an ongoing problem. Even in New Testament times, idols were in vogue. If you lived in Rome, you could worship your choice of gods. The region was like a Super Wal-Mart of deities, each of which you would call on at various times of your life for different needs. You'd need a god for physical healing, a successful crop, safe travel, and even a god to help you through childbirth.[17] (I can't say I'm surprised there was a market for that last one, given that most husbands ... okay, never mind.)

It is against this backdrop that Paul wrote 2 Timothy 3:1–5. Underline the problems in Paul's day that are still an issue for us 2,000 years later.

> But know this: Difficult times will come in the last days. For people will be lovers of self, lovers of money, boastful, proud, blasphemers, disobedient to parents, ungrateful, unholy, unloving, irreconcilable, slanderers, without self-control, brutal, without love for what is good, traitors, reckless, conceited, lovers of pleasure rather than lovers of God, holding to the form of godliness but denying its power. Avoid these people!
>
> (2 TIMOTHY 3:1–5 HCSB)

Sound familiar? It should. It describes America. Below and on the next page are listed some of the descriptions from the passage. After each, note a practical example from today's culture.

Lovers of self:

Lovers of money:

Boastful and proud:

Without self-control:

Without love for what is good:

Lovers of pleasure:

Self. Money. Pride. Evil. Pleasure. Violence. Entitlement. Religious show. America is a pantheon of modern-day gods. What idols do you see in America? What do people prioritize? What has captured the heart of your friends? Your family? Your neighbors? List as many as come to mind.

One particular idol that often needs to be dethroned in my own life is the need for approval. I'm a recovering people-pleaser. Combine that personality trait with my profession as a speaker and writer, and you've got a perfect storm for approval-seeking pursuits. One negative comment on my blog or a negative book review posted on Amazon was enough to send me into a tailspin of self-doubt and insecurity in the past. Fortunately, I have a healthier perspective today and I'm able to resist the common trap of basing my worth on the number of positive comments, likes, followers, or virtual friends I can muster up in a day.

Can you relate? Have you ever asked yourself why it bothers you when a friend or work colleague has more Facebook/Twitter/Instagram friends, followers, likes, or comments than you do?

Perhaps your particular idol doesn't take the shape of a computer. Maybe yours revolves around your need for your children to excel. Cheer captain. Football starter. Academic all-American. Nicely dressed with great manners. Straight teeth. Trendy haircut. Liked by the opposite sex. And if they can quote Scripture, all the better.

Physical perfection. Social status. A title at work. Name-brand clothes. Food. Digits on a scale. Digits on your paycheck. Your husband's accomplishments. Anything that creeps in to steal the primary affection of your heart can be an idol.

What have you made more important than God? What has captured your imagination and energy? Describe the process by which you became enthralled with the created rather than the Creator.

We need to be honest about the idols that tempt us. We need to identify them. We need to stop dancing with the desires of this culture and flirting with false lovers. We need to be honest about their seductive power.

Until then, idols will enslave us, consume us, and ultimately destroy us.

DAY 4: Idolatry = Adultery

We all remember our first love, but chances are, we also remember our first breakup. When my sixth-grade crush asked me to go steady one day after school, I was on cloud nine. Back in my day, it was trendy for a guy to give his steady an ID bracelet with his name on it. It signified that you were chosen, claimed, and off the market, so to speak. (Feminists would have a heyday with the symbolism of that fad!) I proudly wore David's bracelet for a whopping twenty-four hours until he sent his best friend over during lunch period the following day to ask for it back. The next day, another girl was proudly wearing David's bracelet and I was left with a naked wrist and a broken heart. Until of course, Greg asked me to go steady the next week and all was well in the world once again.

We are all in search of true love. A love that will last forever, through the worst of storms and the darkest of nights. Love not based on actions or contingencies, mistakes or emotion. Everyone wants that, right? Even the burliest and toughest of guys long to be loved deep down (but don't tell them that!). Solomon, the wisest man who ever lived and writer of the book of Proverbs (most of it anyway), penned this: "What a person desires is unfailing love" (Proverbs 19:22a).[18] We crave fidelity.

So does God.

So much so that to Him, chasing after idols is more that just rebellion. He sees it as the worst form of infidelity—adultery.

Read: Hosea 1:1–2; 2:2–5; 3:1–5. What emotions do you sense in these passages? Circle them.

Wrathful	Sad	Vengeful	Devastated
Pierced	Angry	Humiliated	Forsaken
Vexed	Crushed	Longing	Betrayed
Frustrated	Mourning	Ashamed	Troubled
Confused	Lonely	Indignant	Enraged

What words and phrases illustrate Israel's rebellion against God? List them below and reference the verses where they are found.

How do these verses change your understanding of God's character?

I took a minute to Google the term "describe God" and my search came back with some interesting results. One website was populated with questions and answers from anyone who would like to respond. Here are some of the answers given:

- Incomprehensible
- Incorporeal
- Eternal
- A supernatural glorified human being
- Uncaring
- Evil

- Omniscient
- Love
- Imaginary
- Energy
- Infinity
- Respectful and perfect friend[19]

A fair percentage of Christians responded with their descriptions, all of which paralleled Scripture; but for the most part, the people who gave an answer defined God in less than stellar terms. Aloof at best, maniacal at worst. And no one came close to portraying God as He is pictured in Hosea: The spurned lover.

God is not an aloof Being unaffected by the actions of the people He created, loved, and died for. God is not indifferent to our rebellion or unmoved by our fickleness. The book of Hosea is filled with the angst and longing of a God who has been wounded by our unfaithfulness to Him. More than just unfaithful, we have been promiscuous (see 6:10 HCSB). In the Hebrew, the word "promiscuity" literally means "whoredom."

That's the whole point of the book of Hosea. Whether you believe Gomer was a real woman or if the whole story is an allegory, the message is the same: God sees our idolatry as adultery, even prostitution, against Himself.

You and I can imagine the anguish a woman would feel if her husband were unfaithful to her. Unfortunately, some of you have experienced it firsthand. The pain would be unbearable; the wound would cut to the core of your heart. Why? Because you gave yourself over to someone, only to have that love betrayed. Tossed aside. A covenant forsaken for a few moments of pleasure.

God has pursued us and has established a covenant with us that He will not break. Yet, we often make light of His love and affection, His passion and ardor for us. We toss aside His love to follow after idols that take the place of importance that only He deserves. We forsake Him for a few moments of pleasure. Over and over again. Like a woman who sells her body for a meal and some money, we give ourselves over and over to anything that promises to fill our souls.

Why would we do that? Perhaps because we don't think God can fill the empty places in our hearts and souls. Maybe it's because we don't really believe God loves us. We've reasoned that He surely can't love us deeply enough to be hurt by our faithless actions; maybe, deep down, we have bought into the lie that God is untouchable, unreachable.

But He's not. Hosea's story proves it. So does Calvary.

Our idolatry, our adultery, breaks God's heart.

DAY 5: Too Good . . . but True

I've often joked that by the time I arrived at the foot of the cross at the age of twenty-one, there was a fleet of U-haul trucks behind me ready and waiting to unload my sins. I could hardly believe the good news that because of Jesus' death, my debt was forgiven and my sins were nailed to the cross, as Paul said in Colossians 2:13–14.

Perhaps your journey to the foot of the cross was smoother and your sin list shorter. You might have decided to follow Jesus during VBS as a kindergartener or at your parents' bedside when you were in second grade. If so, you might not fully appreciate the drama that unfolds in the book of Hosea. The message may seem like just another plea for repentance from one of the prophets. After all, that's what all the prophets spoke about. Repent. Turn back. Find forgiveness. Praise God. Yada, yada, yada.

For some, though, the offer at the cross seems just too good to be true. A pipe dream. A cruel joke.

For a moment, I want you to think about what it might have been like to be Gomer. Scripture tells us that when Hosea meets her, she has already been promiscuous (Hosea 1:2). She's a prostitute. That same verse tells us that she will have children conceived from her sexual encounters. This is a deeply troubled woman. Hosea 3:1 tells us that Gomer left Hosea and went to be with someone else. Because verse 3 states that Hosea "bought her for fifteen shekels of silver," some scholars think she had become a slave.[20] That's how completely destitute and desperate she had become.

Prostitute. Harlot. Slave. Used (and probably abused) by men and scorned by women. An outcast. Unclean. Despised. Rejected. Dejected. Desperate. Can you feel her emptiness? Her shame? Can you see how she would think that true love, grace, mercy, forgiveness could never, ever apply to her? She'd gone too far, done too much.

But that's exactly what Hosea offered to her:

> I [Hosea] said to her, "You must live with me many days. Don't be promiscuous or belong to any man, and I will act the same way toward you."
>
> (HOSEA 3:3 HSCB)

Can you imagine Gomer's disbelief? If you've ever found yourself enslaved to sin, destroyed by it and betrayed by it, you understand. Can I really believe that God would forgive me? After all I've done? Perhaps that's why so many people can't believe that God's love is unconditional. But it is. That's what He was trying to communicate through Hosea to the people of Israel—and to us.

Read: Hosea 14. In the left column, list the phrases or sentences that called Israel (and us) to turn back to Him. In the right column, jot down the promises God offered if the people would repent.

Call to Repentance	Promises of Restoration

Look again at verses 8–9. What do these verses have in common? What do they say about the results of continued rebellion against God?

I love how *The Message* paraphrases Hosea 14:8:

> Ephraim is finished with gods that are no-gods.
>> From now on I'm the one who answers and satisfies him.
> I am like a luxuriant fruit tree.
>> Everything you need is to be found in me.

Isn't that the message of this chapter? The message of the entire book of Hosea?

Idols cannot answer the deepest questions of our hearts. False gods cannot satisfy us. Anything this world has to offer will only leave us wanting more, something that will ease the ache in our souls. Everything we need, truly need, can only be found in relationship with God through Christ. We can chase after other lovers, only to find the sheets cold and the bed empty the next morning.

Say goodbye to those false loves. Return to the Lover of your soul.

His arms are open. His heart is love. He waits for you.

Move On Challenge

Find time this week to list the idols or false gods that most often displace God in your order of affections. Write a thank-you note to God that begins with a sincere confession of your habit of chasing other gods. Now, take a few minutes to picture yourself on the auction block and God showing up to buy your freedom in spite of your disloyalty. End your note by pouring out the gratitude you feel toward Him.

Falling Forward

I find the great thing in this world is not so much where
we stand as in what direction we are moving.
To reach the port of heaven, we must sail sometimes with the wind
and sometimes against it —
but we must sail, and not drift, nor lie at anchor.

OLIVER WENDELL HOLMES

Welcome

Welcome to the final session of *Move On: When Mercy Meets Your Mess*. Before watching the video, briefly discuss with each other what has been happening in your lives during the week. Also discuss any key points that stood out to you from the between-sessions personal study and any questions that came up since the last session.

Video Teaching

As you watch the video for session six, use the following outline to record any thoughts or concepts that stand out to you.

When the early pioneers found themselves stuck in a rut, they unloaded their wagons to lighten the burden and started pushing. How many of us remain in spiritual ruts because we fail to unload our original burdens and push forward?

One of the biggest challenges we will face in the Christian journey is to resist the temptation to drift or—even worse—allow the current to carry us off course.

The goal for which we strive each day is choosing to follow Christ despite the temptation of sin and the trials of life. Jesus, in all His glory and perfection, stands waiting for us at the end of the journey.

It's awfully hard to stretch forward when we've assumed the posture of a face plant on the track or relegated ourselves to sitting on the sidelines. There will be interruptions in the race, but we can't allow those roadblocks to stall our journey.

Some people fall *down*, while others fall *forward*. Those who simply fall down make getting back up their primary goal. Those who fall forward make crossing the finish line their primary focus.

When we fall forward, we don't look around and compare ourselves to the other runners in the race or try to measure up to their progress. We keep our line of vision solely on the finish line.

Moving on is only possible when our hearts are yielded to Christ and we rely on His mercy and perfection.

The greatest need for us as God's people is to live up to what we already have in Christ. We cannot allow our imperfections, stumbling steps, or hurdles to get the best of us, because we know the race has already been won.

God wants to use our messes as part of His bigger story. Our life purpose is to testify to the gospel and the grace of God.

Small Group Discussion

Take some time at this point to discuss with your fellow group members what you just watched and to explore these concepts in Scripture.

1. In the introduction to this session, I explain how the early pioneers would travel dirt roads in covered wagons and literally get "stuck in a rut." Their choice was to stay put or figure out a way to free themselves and move on. How is this similar to the choices we face when confronted with spiritual ruts and setbacks in our journey?

2. What are some of the ruts in which you have found yourself? What tends to bog you down and leave you feeling helpless and defeated?

3. **Read:** Philippians 3:12–16. What was Paul's ultimate goal? What two things did he do to reach for that prize?

4. How is continually pressing on to reach our goal a mark of spiritual maturity?

5. Would you describe yourself as someone who is more likely to fall down or fall forward when encountering various difficulties in life's race? Why?

6. We began this study by looking at the need for us to let ourselves off the hook when it comes to being perfect. As you reflect on what we've covered during the past six weeks, in what ways have you been tempted to try to run a "perfect" race? How have you now committed to allow God's mercy to meet you in your mess?

Closing Prayer

Close your time together in prayer. Here are a few ideas on what you and your group members can pray based on the topic of this session:

○ Pray that God will show you your spiritual ruts and help you unload your burdens on Him.

○ Pray that God will enable you to "fall forward" and overcome the challenges that come your way.

○ Pray that God will help you keep focused on Him at all times—not on your own progress or the progress of others.

○ Pray that you will realize the inheritance you have in Christ and allow God to use your messes as part of His bigger story.

Recommended Reading

Review chapter 10, "Falling Forward," in *Move On: When Mercy Meets Your Mess.* Use the space below to write any key points or questions, and take some time this week to share these with a fellow group member. Also reflect with that person on how God has guided you during this study to help you confront your messes, take them to God, and move on.

Some give up their designs when they have almost reached the goal;
while others, on the contrary, obtain a victory by exerting,
at the last moment, more vigorous efforts than before.

POLYBIUS

Final Personal Study

DAY 1: Fall Out or Fall Forward

When babies learn to walk, they are going to have their fair share of spills until they become steadier on their wobbly feet. I had forgotten how hard it is to watch this process until my grandson began to take his first steps. My instinct, like many other mothers, was to rush around in front of him, clearing his path along the way and lean in every time he made a move. I seriously looked like I was playing offense at a basketball game, throwing my arms in front of any obstacle to guard my fellow teammate as he dribbled the ball toward the hoop. It was a bit over the top. And heaven forbid, if the poor lad happened to fall, it was Mimi to the rescue! I would swoop in and scoop that baby up like a fighter jet on a rescue mission. I all but promised him a pony in an attempt to thwart his oncoming tears.

All of us—from the anonymous widow in your church to Billy Graham—know what it's like to fall down, metaphorically speaking. It's a part of the Christian journey; none of us is exempt. The sting of skinning our spiritual knees on a stronghold. A word misspoken. An idol that has captured our attention and our hearts.

The disciples were no different, especially Peter. Considered one of Jesus' closest allies, this fisherman-turned-fisher of men experienced his share of glorious victories as well as stunning defeats, the most infamous of which is his denial of Jesus. If you're not familiar with the story, read up on it now in Mark 14:66–72.

Picture yourself in Peter's place. How would you have responded after having denied Jesus? Where would you go? What would you do?

Scripture tells us that after the crucifixion, Peter did what felt natural and seemed logical: he went fishing. The Bible doesn't record what was going on in Peter's mind and heart, but we can guess pretty accurately because we've all felt the same way when we've fallen short of God's design for our lives—defeated, discouraged, desperate, disillusioned, ashamed. But, the Savior who had just redeemed the world through His death and resurrection was about to redeem Peter's heart and mission.

Read: John 21:15–22. Jesus and His disciples had just shared a meal together, a custom that demonstrated relationship and fellowship. On the heels of this meal, Jesus spoke directly to Peter. Why do you think Jesus repeatedly asked Peter if he loved Him?

Why do you think Jesus added the phrase "more than these" in verse 15?

What "these" do you think Jesus was referencing?

What was Peter's response to the questions?

How do you think Peter felt during this conversation?

Why do you think Peter asked about John's future?

How do we know that Peter accepted Jesus' forgiveness, restoration, and commission?

Peter faced a choice. He could either remain a fisherman and live out his days in regret and shame, or he could embrace the grace and forgiveness of Jesus and live out his days telling the known world about the Messiah who rose from the dead. He could live in the past or in the present, but he couldn't do both. With his knees scraped up, his pride wounded, and his self-centered bravado stripped away, he faced a choice. He could fall out or fall forward. He could base his future on the sum of his past mistakes, or he could embrace the present and base his future on God's calling on his life.

When you and I fall on our faces—and we will—we face the same choice. To fall out or fall forward. To repent or quit. To trust in God's mercy and grace to finish the race, or drop out of the race altogether.

Jesus has forgiven you and has set you back up on your feet.

Will you move forward?

DAY 2: **The Blame Game**

There's one in every bunch. If you're a mom, you've probably intersected paths with the naïve mother who refuses to believe her precious child could do any wrong. I encountered one such mother years ago. Her teenage son had hosted a party at their house when they were out of town and there were plenty of pictures on Facebook to attest to the fact. However, when presented with the evidence by another mother, the mother refused to believe her son was to blame.

"That just doesn't sound like something he would do. There is no way he would initiate anything like that."

"He told me that some upperclassmen found out we (the parents) were out of town and they showed up with alcohol unannounced and uninvited."

"He didn't know what to do, but he prayed everyone would leave."

And my personal favorite: "He said he took up the car keys of anyone who was driving to keep them from getting on the roads." Puhleese.

Never mind that the young man in question had texted his friends to come over and invite others to join them. Never mind that there were plenty of pictures of the young man consuming alcohol and enjoying the revelry in his home. Never mind that he threw everyone else under the bus to protect himself.

Bless his mother's heart for refusing to face the facts. She certainly didn't do her son any favors by allowing him to participate in the "blame game."

Shirking responsibility for our actions comes naturally to us. In fact, our spiritual ancestors were pros. Adam blamed Eve for eating the forbidden fruit. Aaron said the golden calf just jumped out of the fire all by itself. The devil made me do it. It's all her fault. He forced my hand.

Sound familiar?

In the Old Testament, Saul blamed Samuel for sinning against God. **Read:** 1 Samuel 10:8. What did Samuel command Saul to do and NOT to do?

Now **read** 1 Samuel 13:1–14. Describe the situation at hand in these verses.

How did the Israelites respond to the presence of the Philistines?

What do verses 7–8 tell us?

What did Saul do when Samuel didn't show up when Saul wanted him to?

How did Saul explain his actions? Whom did he blame? Why?

What was Samuel's respond to Saul's excuses?

    I can understand Saul's fear. After all, he was the first king of Israel and he was in a difficult position. He was facing a fortified Philistine army "as numerous as the sand on the seashore" (v. 5). His measly army of 2,000 was headed for the hills, deserting him out of fear. I'd be scared too.

    Rather than following God's command to wait for Samuel to offer the sacrifice, Saul took matters into his own hands. He offered the sacrifice in direct contradiction to the Lord's instruction. "Just as he finished making the offering" (v. 10), Samuel showed up. And the blame game began.

    The troops were deserting me.

    You didn't come when you said you would.

    The Philistines were gathering.

I had no choice. I had to offer the sacrifice.

Nowhere in this story did Saul actually admit his sin as sin. And as a result, Saul's kingdom was ripped from him and given to David. God cared more about Saul's disobedience than a threatening Philistine army (which was later defeated). Disobeying God is serious business.

I wonder what would have happened if Saul had simply confessed his sin instead of blaming everyone else around him. I wonder if God would have allowed him more success and a longer reign. Unfortunately, Saul spiraled downward into a pit of desperation so deep that he even tried to kill his own son. Some even claimed he was crazy. Sad.

When God confronts you (or me) in your sin, you have a choice: You can blame everyone else around you and shift the responsibility away from yourself, or you can come clean and admit your sin. You can try to hide (like Adam and Eve), or you can ask God to create in you a clean heart (like David; see Psalm 51). One will leave you on the sideline with Saul, stuck in your sin. The other will bring you liberation from sin and the chance to start over again.

It's the difference between falling away and falling forward.

DAY 3: One Step Forward

Truth or Dare. For most of us, it's a childhood rite of passage. I don't know about you, but I was always the girl to take the dare. I would rather swallow a teaspoonful of vanilla extract or prank-call the school principal than have to divulge who my current crush was or fess up to my first kiss (which ironically can be traced back to a game of Spin the Bottle!). A dare, no matter how absurd, has a shorter life span. It's over and done with, while the truth, if confessed, sticks around to haunt you in the days to follow. At least that was my reasoning.

In a similar manner, we play the same game with God. We've learned over the years to cordon off parts of our hearts and lives to Him. There are darkened places of sin and strongholds, embarrassing moments we'd rather forget. And we are afraid of what God would say to us if we were honest with Him about those places in our hearts. We know He knows about them, but we can't imagine having to verbally acknowledge or confess them.

However, the only way to move forward in our relationship with Him involves us opening those doors, removing the bars, and coming clean with our sin. It's a process called confession.

Read: 1 John 1:8–2:2. What is the result of denying sin?

What is the result of confessing sin?

When we do sin, how does Jesus act on our behalf?

What is Jesus called in 1 John 2:2 (according to the KJV and the HCSB)? And what does that mean?

I'm not sure why we try to cover up our sin. Scripture makes it clear that we're all sinners (Romans 3:23). Perhaps it's just old-fashioned pride. Or embarrassment at how easily we are tempted and lured away into sin. Or both. Regardless, all of us are sinners. Sanctified sinners. Justified sinners. But sinners still.

John made it clear that denying sin shows that we are just fooling ourselves and demonstrating to others that God's truth hasn't penetrated our hearts.

But oh, dear friend, when we move past our own pride and confess our sins, not only do we have a clean heart and clean hands, but we have an

Advocate who goes before God on our behalf. Someone who will speak on our behalf and in our place. When we sin, it's as if Jesus is at the throne saying, "I've died for her. She is forgiven." He is our "propitiation." That word isn't used much in the New Testament. It means that Jesus' death appeased or turned away God's divine wrath against sin.

Because of what Jesus accomplished on the cross, we can experience God's forgiveness when we sin rather than His wrath. Rather than bear the consequences of our rebellion against God, we can know His mercy and grace. Rather than *fear* God, we can come *near* to God in our time of need (Hebrews 4:16). That's what confession is all about.

Confession clears away the junk in our hearts that keeps us from a deeper, richer, stronger fellowship with God. It allows us to "throw off" ("lay aside," HCSB) every sin that snares our feet (Hebrews 12:1) and keeps us from moving forward.

What unconfessed sin is keeping you on the sidelines instead of in the race?

What are you ashamed of admitting before God?

Jesus is waiting as your Advocate. God wants to cleanse you.

What are you waiting for? It's time to move forward.

DAY 4: **Who Do You Think You Are?**

From 1988 to 2011, I had at least one child in the nest. Twenty-three years of clocking in as a full-time mom. Nurturing skinned knees and hurt feelings; juggling ball practices, carpool duties, and school projects. It was hard to imagine a day would come when I would be relieved of my full-time duties. And just as suddenly as it all began, it came to a screeching halt on the day my husband and I moved our youngest child into a college dorm to begin his freshman year. It just so happened to also be the same year his two older siblings got married. I went from full-time to part-time to "call me when you need some wash done or run out of money." Oh boy, was it hard. Like many other mothers, my identity had been so wrapped up in my children and their various activities that it was a struggle to figure out who I was supposed to be in the next chapter of my life.

In today's culture that likes to put labels on everyone for ease of relating to or dismissing others, we women often struggle with our identity. Have you ever wondered to yourself: who am I, really? When all of the labels are stripped off, who am I? Have you ever thought to yourself, "I wouldn't know what to do with myself if I didn't have to shuttle the kids, teach a class at church, finish a project at work, or tackle piles of laundry"? We often buy into the deadly myth that who we are is based on what we do, what noble pursuits we pursue.

So who are you? How would you answer that question? Take some time to reflect.

Could you answer the question without saying, "I'm a wife, a mom, a teacher, a Bible study leader, I'm a ... "?

Could you answer the question without defining yourself based on what you do on a daily basis?

Why do we struggle with this so much?

Because we live in a world that tells us that we are the sum of what we do—good or bad. The woman who had an affair and everyone in the church found out. The mom who is obsessed with nutrition and staying in shape. That helicopter mom who hovers over every detail of her children's lives. That woman who has a bestselling book or a popular blog. The lady at church with the nice car and huge house.

The inherent problem with this means of identity is that who we are can change at any moment. What if you get fired? What if you gain weight? What happens when your kids decide to quit playing soccer? Or graduate from high school? What happens when you fall on your face in moral failure? Who are you after your husband leaves you? How would you define yourself on a day when you yell at your kids in frustration? Who are you when the applause fades and you are alone?

Scripture provides us with answers for those questions. Remember, though, that Scripture doesn't always tell you what you want. It is Truth.

Read the following Scriptures and draw lines to match them to the descriptions they provide.

John 1:12	A glorious crown
Ephesians 1:7	His possession
2 Corinthians 5:17	The righteousness of God
Ephesians 2:10	A new creation
2 Corinthians 5:21	Child of God
1 Peter 2:9	Redeemed
Isaiah 62:3	His workmanship

What do all of these descriptions have in common?

All of the descriptions are bestowed on you by God Almighty. You didn't do anything to deserve them, so you can't do anything to lose them. Even when you fall. Flat. On. Your. Face. You are still His glorious crown. You are still a child of God. Even when it seems like you're anything but a reflection of Him, you are still His workmanship.

God does not define you by your sins or your successes, your feats or your failures, your accomplishment or your atrocities.

He defines you by His love and His work in your life.

And that, dear friend, is enough.

DAY 5: **Remembering to Remember**

"Remember when ... ?"

For me, that task is getting a bit more difficult with every birthday. These days it's a struggle to remember why I walked into a room. Was it to grab something? Turn off something? Put something away? Who knows? I give up.

Remembering is important for things like finding your keys (usually lurking in a hidden abyss of my purse) or finding your reading glasses (usually on top of my head). It's much, much more critical in matters of faith and falling forward.

Read: Deuteronomy 8:1–14. Describe the setting. (You may need to skim earlier chapters.)

List any verses that use the words "remember" or "do not forget" or "keep in mind."

Why did God command them to remember? How was remembering a good thing for the people of Israel?

From what you know of biblical history, were the people of Israel good at remembering how God had moved in their lives and in their ancestors' lives? Explain.

In the NIV, the word "remember" occurs 166 times.[21] Let's not forget all the "do not forget" references (I didn't try to look those up). To put it into perspective, the word "marriage" is mentioned only 43 times,[22] and the term "money" is used just 121 times.[23]

Why would God continually prompt us to remember?

Because it's really easy to forget.

When we fail, fall flat, mess up, and generally disappoint ourselves, we forget how far God has brought us. We forget how God has changed our lives. We forget that our sin does not define us. We forget that while we are on this planet, we will sin. We will disappoint others. And ourselves. We will stumble and tumble and trip and spill and stagger and lurch and wobble. And fall. Hard.

Remembering is critical if you want to move on and move forward, fall forward instead of falling down.

- Remembering offers us encouragement—We can forget what is behind (Philippians 3:13).

- Remembering fuels our hope—God will continue to work in us (Philippians 1:6).

- Remembering gives us the right perspective—It's all about God and not about us (Galatians 1:3–5).

- Remembering heightens our anticipation—When we see Him, we will be like Him (1 John 3:2).

- Remembering anchors us—We are a part of a much larger story (Hebrews 11).

- Remembering drives our courage—The same God who was present then goes with us now, so we can face whatever comes (Joshua 1:9).

Moving forward means looking back. Not in order to discourage us, but rather to spark our incentive to keep going.

Climbing in the mountains can be an arduous feat. You're up against rocks, roots, tree branches, snakes, and a hundred other things that challenge your ascent. Your legs ache, your lungs scream for air, and you just don't know if you want to take another step. So you stop and look back. You take note of how far the trail has brought you. You may not be at the top, but your vantage point provides enough glimpses of what you'll see in the end that you keep going. And you stop and glance. And start again.

That's what remembering does for us. The Christian life can be an arduous journey. You're up against people and situations and temptations that challenge your desire to keep going forward. Your heart screams for relief and you can't catch your breath in the midst of the trials that seem to go on forever. So you stop and look back. Remember. You take note of how far God has brought you. You're not there—heaven is yet ahead—but He provides enough glimpses of glory, enough grace for yourself and others, enough courage to trust in the unseen. So you keep going. You move forward. One step at a time.

Don't give up on the journey. Don't let your circumstances derail you. Don't let your sin define you. Don't let others discourage you. Put one foot in front of the other and ... move on.

Move On Challenge

Spend some time in focused prayer and ask God to reveal to you the barriers that hinder you from moving on in the Christian journey. Are you stuck due to an ongoing struggle or heartbreak? Is it an area of your past or something that continues to leave you burdened with shame? Maybe your faith has been stalled due to a mindset of "us and them" or legalistic thinking. Or maybe you're distracted by false gods that have stolen the affection you once had for God. Or perhaps, an area of sin has steered you off course and you are desperate to get back on track. As you are honest before God, list on the left below the areas that hinder you from "falling forward." Then, beside each one, list at least one action step you plan to take in the days ahead in an effort to move forward in your journey of faith. At the bottom of your list, write in big, bold letters: MOVING ON.

Endnotes

1. Blue Letter Bible, "*balah*," Strong's # H1086. http://www.blueletterbible.org/lang/lexicon/lexicon.cfm?Strongs=H1086&t=KJV.

2. American Society of Plastic Surgeons, "2012 Quick Facts." http://www.plasticsurgery.org/Documents/news-resources/statistics/2012-Plastic-Surgery-Statistics/plastic-surgery-trends-quick-facts.pdf.

3. Ibid.

4. "100 Million Dieters, $20 Billion: The Weight-loss Industry by the Numbers," ABC News, May 8, 2012. http://abcnews.go.com/Health/100-million-dieters-20-billion-weight-loss-industry/story?id=16297197.

5. "The Price of Hunger," *Los Angeles Times*, June 23, 2008. http://articles.latimes.com/2008/jun/23/opinion/ed-food23.

6. "Kudzu," University of Florida Center for Aquatic and Invasive Plants, 2008. http://plants.ifas.ufl.edu/node/354.

7. "Kudzu," Missouri Department of Conservation, June 20, 2011. http://mdc.mo.gov/sites/default/files/resources/2011/06/kudzusheet_06-30-11.pdf.

8. "Kudzu," USDA Forest Service, Forest Health Staff, October 12, 2004. http://www.na.fs.fed.us/fhp/invasive_plants/weeds/kudzu.pdf.

9. "Kudzu," Washington Invasive Species Council, 2009. http://www.invasivespecies.wa.gov/priorities/kudzu.shtml.

10. Blue Letter Bible, "condemn; condemnation," from the *International Standard Bible Encylopaedia*. http://www.blueletterbible.org/search/Dictionary/viewTopic.cfm?topic=IT0002251.

11. Blue Letter Bible, "*nyn*," Strong's # G3568, http://www.blueletterbible.org/lang/lexicon/lexicon.cfm?Strongs=G3568&t=NIV.

12. James Orr, gen. ed., "Gentiles," *International Standard Bible Encyclopedia*, 1915. http://www.biblestudytools.com/encyclopedias/isbe/gentiles.html.

13. "Where Is the Deepest Place on Earth," Wonderopolis. http://wonderopolis.org/wonder/where-is-the-deepest-place-on-earth/#sthash.jFndOKdP.dpuf.

14. See 1 Samuel 5:2; 1 Kings 11:5, 7; 18:18–19; 2 Kings 5:18; 17:30–31; 19:37; Isaiah 46:1; Ezekiel 8:14.

15. Blue Letter Bible, "jealous." http://www.blueletterbible.org/search/search.cfm?Criteria=jealous%2A+H7067&t=KJV#s=s_primary_0_1.

16. Ibid., *"qanna,"* Strong's #H 7067. http://www.blueletterbible.org/lang/lexicon/lexicon.cfm?Strongs=H7067&t=KJV.

17. Paula Fredriksen, "The Empire's Religions," *Frontline*, PBS, April 1998. http://www.pbs.org/wgbh/pages/frontline/shows/religion/portrait/empire.html#cult.

18. A. R. Fausset, "The Book of Proverbs," Blue Letter Bible. http://www.blueletterbible.org/Comm/jfb/Pro/Pro_000.cfm?a=647001.

19. "How Do U Describe God?" Yahoo! Answers. http://answers.yahoo.com/question/index?qid=20100405034134AAiXjsq.

20. Chuck Smith, "Series on Hosea 1–4," Blue Letter Bible. http://www.blueletterbible.org/Comm/smith_chuck/c2000_Hsa/Hsa_001.cfm?a=865002.

21. Blue Letter Bible, "remember." http://www.blueletterbible.org/search/search.cfm?Criteria=remember&t=NIV#s=s_primary_0_.

22. Ibid., "marriage." http://www.blueletterbible.org/search/search.cfm?Criteria=marriage&t=NIV#s=s_primary_0_1.

23. Ibid., "money." http://www.blueletterbible.org/search/search.cfm?Criteria=money&t=NIV#s=s_primary_0_1.

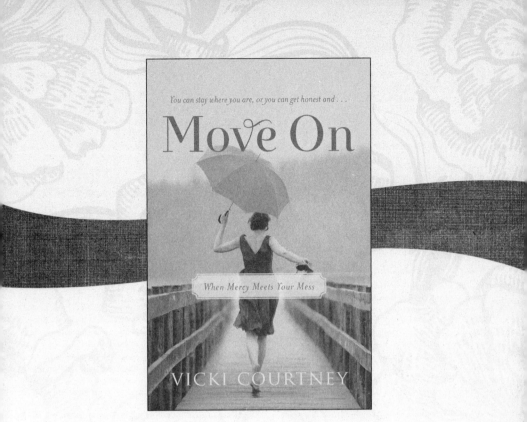

You can stay where you are, or you can get honest and . . .

Move On

When Mercy Meets Your Mess

VICKI COURTNEY

Life is often messy. God makes provision to help us move beyond our messes, but often our first instinct is to hide, deny, ignore, or run from them. Yet it is in the middle of our mess where mercy shows up and offers a safe place to process our struggles, imperfections, doubts, and fears. Then, with mercy by our side, we are able to move on and experience the grace and freedom God intended.

In *Move On*, best-selling author Vicki Courtney helps readers come clean with their muddy messes, revealing the deeper issues they must face, including:

- *Christian snobbery*
- *struggles and broken dreams*
- *the past*
- *shame*

- *legalism*
- *the need for approval*
- *idols*
- *fickle faith*

Once we face our messes, God, with his sweet mercy, can help us to get real, deal, and truly move on.